Vegetarian for a Day

Laureen Osborne

PublishAmerica
Baltimore

© 2010 by Laureen Osborne.
All rights reserved. No part of this book may be reproduced, stored in a retrieval system or transmitted in any form or by any means without the prior written permission of the publishers, except by a reviewer who may quote brief passages in a review to be printed in a newspaper, magazine or journal.

First printing

PublishAmerica has allowed this work to remain exactly as the author intended, verbatim, without editorial input.

Hardcover 978-1-4489-3531-4
Softcover 978-1-60610-327-2
PUBLISHED BY PUBLISHAMERICA, LLLP
www.publishamerica.com
Baltimore

Printed in the United States of America

Table of Contents

Introduction 7
How to Use This Cookbook 9
Cooking Terms 11
Cooking Tips 13
Healthy Eating: The Vegetarian Diet 14
The Protein Myth 16
10 Tips for Healthy Eating 20
The Vegetarian Pantry 21
Tools of the Trade 27
Introduction to Legumes (Beans, Peas and Lentils) 31
Introduction to Grains 34
Introduction to Nuts & Seeds 38
Legumes and Grains: Legume Recipes 39
Bean Burritos 41
Bean Burgers 43
Bean Chili 45
Bean & Cheese Quesadillas 47
Bean & Rice Burgers 49
Beans in Tomato Sauce 52
Black Bean Biryani 54
Black Beans & Rice 56
Chick Peas in Tahini Sauce 58
Cucumber Raita 60
Curried Chick Peas 61
Dahl 62
Falafel—Recipe #1 64
Falafel—Recipe #2 67
Lentil Biryani 69

Lentil Loaf	72
Rice and Beans	74
Spicy Chick Peas	76
Spinach and Lentils	78
Legumes and Grains: Grain Recipes	81
Italian Polenta	83
Mexican Spoon Bread	86
Quinoa	88
Stuffed Peppers	89
Vegetable Biryani	91
Introduction to Meat Alternatives	93
Meat Alternatives: Recipes	95
Burritos	97
Italian Meatballs	100
Laureen's Chili	102
"Meat" Sauce	105
Pineapple Meatballs	108
Stroganoff	111
Sweet & Sour Cabbage Rolls	113
Introduction to Vegetables	115
Vegetables: Recipes	119
Bok Choi Stir Fry	121
Broccoli Bake	123
Cauliflower Casserole	124
Eggplant Parmesana	128
Fried Eggplant	130
Gourmet Pizza	132
Indian Spinach & Potato Balls with Spicy Yoghurt Sauce	141
Moroccan Vegetable Stew	144
Onion Tart	147
Oriental Noodle Salad	150
Roasted Vegetables with Pasta	152
Singapore Fried Vermicelli	154
Spanakopita	157
Thai Curry Stew	159
Vegetable Curry	162

Vegetarian Stew	164
Winter Vegetable Stew	166
Introduction to Tofu	168
Stir Frying	171
Tofu: Recipes	175
Baked Tofu	177
Noodle Soup	179
Spicy Bean Curd	182
Tofu Loaf	185
Tofu with Ginger Sauce	187
Introduction to Pasta	189
Pasta: Recipes	191
Arrabiata Sauce	193
Asian Noodle Salad	194
Broccoli Sauce	197
Coriander Sauce	199
Dill Sauce	201
Fettuccine Alfredo	203
Fresh Tomato Sauce	206
Lasagna with "Meat" Filling	208
Macaroni and Cheese	212
Marinara Sauce	213
"Meaty" Sauce	214
Mushroom Lasagna	216
Mushroom Manicotti	218
Mushroom Sauce	221
Pasta Salad	223
Pesto Sauce	225
Rose Sauce	227
Spinach Lasagna	229
Introduction to Eggs & Cheese	232
Egg and Cheese: Recipes	235
Cheese Quesadillas	237
Egg Foo Young	239
Eggs Benedict	241
Huevos Rancheros	243

"Italian" Style Eggs	**245**
Mushroom Frittata	**247**
Mushroom Quiche	**250**
Paneer with Spinach	**252**
Potato and Onion Frittata	**255**
Vegetarian for a Day	258
Becoming a Vegetarian	259
About the Author	260
Endnotes	261
Bibliography and References	263

Introduction

The prevalence of fad diets, diet books and weight loss clinics that have sprung up across North America in the last couple of years tells us one thing: we are concerned about our bodies.

In North America we are facing an obesity crisis. 2/3 of all Americans have a body weight above healthy levels. In 1998 17.9% of all Americans were considered obese, that number reached 20% in 2000. In Canada, statistics for 1998 showed 14.8% of the adult population was obese. That number in 2001 is now 15%. Obesity is measured in terms of BMI (Body Mass Index)[1]

In addition to eating less, we now know we have to eat better. This means lowering our fat intake and increasing our fiber.

Now, for some good news—by eating just one vegetarian meal a week, you will be taking an important step towards a healthier diet! Did you know?—

a Vegetarian diet is typically low in fat and high in fiber

a Vegetarian diet helps you lose weight because a higher fiber intake helps you feel full while eating less food!

a Vegetarian diet includes lots of fruits and vegetables. Fruits and vegetables contain vitamins and minerals and are also high in Antioxidants, which are thought to prevent cancer[2] . Antioxidants fight diseases which compromise the immune system.

Let's discuss some of the common misconceptions people have about eating vegetarian:

Myth: *Vegetarians don't eat enough Protein*—"How can they stay alive just eating vegetables?"!!

Fact: The fact is most North Americans eat **too much** protein. The body uses what it needs for energy and the rest is stored.

Myth: Vegetarian food is boring—"I couldn't stand eating bean sprouts and tofu all day!"

Fact: Some of the most wonderful food in the world comes from predominantly vegetarian cultures such as India and the Far East. Their seasonings and herbs make recipes tasty and exotic.

Myth: It takes too long to prepare a Vegetarian Meal!

Fact: I can usually get a delicious vegetarian meal on the table in 30 minutes. I use canned legumes instead of dried (legumes are lentils, chick peas, kidney beans, etc.). Stir frying is one of the fastest cooking methods in the world. Vegetarian stews prepared in the pressure cooker are ready in about three minutes!

Indian, Thai and Chinese food are now very popular and most supermarkets have a specialty food aisle. There you will find ready made sauces. All you do is add your ingredients, heat and serve—what could be quicker?!

Chances are you are all ready eating vegetarian meals without even realizing it. Have you ever had spaghetti with Marinara or Prima Vera sauce? or Pizza with mushrooms and green pepper? How about an all-time favorite "comfort food" macaroni and cheese?!

This book has been designed to introduce you to the concept of "vegetarian" eating. After sampling a few recipes, you will notice that you haven't missed meat, you feel satisfied and every meal is delicious.

How to Use This Cookbook

Set aside one evening a week to make a vegetarian meal. Try to choose a night when the whole family is together so that everyone can "Go Vegetarian." When doing your meal planning for the week, flip through the book and choose a recipe.

Most of the recipes in this book can be prepared and about ½ an hour. There are many things you can do to save time in the preparation of vegetarian meals including:

Buy canned legumes instead of dried—they are ready to use. Simply drain and rinse under cold water

Always cut fresh vegetables uniformly and thinly so they cook evenly and fast

"Pre-cooking" vegetables (either by steaming, sautéing or microwaving) as suggested in some of the recipes, will greatly reduce your overall cooking time

"Mise en Place" is a French cooking term meaning "put in place." It means having everything at hand to prepare a meal before you start cooking. Assemble all your ingredients, pre-measure quantities and pre-cut vegetables. You will find this method of meal preparation will save you a lot of time—and you won't accidentally forget an ingredient!

Use "Garbage Bowls" save yourself a few steps and toss all your "green" refuse into a big, handy bowl. Material can later be transferred to your composter. Use a second bowl for other items such as cans, boxes and wrappers which can later be put in the appropriate recycle bins in your home.

The ingredient list may give you a choice of 1 or 2 quantity. If you're not sure about the quantity, always choose the lesser amount; you can always add more the next time you prepare the dish—this is important to remember if the quantity refers to a spice such as hot peppers or chili peppers.

The ingredient list may give you "Optional" ingredients—if an optional ingredients adds heat to the dish, and you're not sure you will like it, leave it out.

The ingredient list often includes garnishes—these too are optional. They serve two purposes: they add another layer of flavor and make for a more attractive presentation.

Cooking Terms

There are a few terms used in the book that you should familiarize yourself with:

Beat means to mix vigorously with a spoon, fork, or beater
Caramelize To heat over low heat until the food turns a golden brown color
Chiffonade A technique of cutting tender, easily bruised leaves into thin strips without damaging the leaf
Chop   To cut food into smaller pieces
Dice   To cut food into equal-sized pieces, ¼" or less, like cubes
Julienne   To cut into long thin strips
Marinate   Marinate is to let food soak in a prepared liquid to add flavor and tenderize
Mince   (garlic) chopping into very, very tiny pieces
Sauté   To cook food quickly in a small amount of fat or oil until brown, in a skillet or sauté pan over direct heat. The pan and oil *must* be hot before adding the food or the food will absorb the oil and become soggy
Simmer   To cook in liquid almost to boiling, but not hot enough to bubble
Smash   (e.g. garlic) lay the clove of garlic on your cutting board and place the broadest part of your Chef's knife or cleaver on top of the clove. Using the heel of your hand, "smash" the blade down on top of the clove, breaking it up. The clove can be used like this or more often, finely chopped or diced
Whisk   Is to use a whisk utensil to mix or beat ingredients thoroughly

You will find that cooking vegetarian meals takes very little time and you will be rewarded with the knowledge that you have made a healthy choice for yourself, your family and the planet.

Bon Appetit!

Cooking Tips

To prepare basil, take the individual leaves off the stem and tightly roll them cigar style. Using a sharp knife, cut the rolls into small strips and add the basil to your dish. The flavor will be stronger if they are added just before stirring.

Keep a large bowl on your counter for garbage

Use the French "*Mise En Place*" method of food preparation: before beginning your dish, assembly all the ingredients you will be using. Pre-chop and measure before beginning. Place ingredients on a large plate or tray and you're ready to go!

Freeze onions for about 10-15 minutes before cutting them and you won't cry!

Leftover tomato paste can be frozen right in the can—simply remove both ends of the can before placing in the freezer. When you need some, push the required amount out of the can, and return the rest to the freezer.

Healthy Eating: The Vegetarian Diet

Both the U.S. and Canadian governments recommend the following guidelines for healthy eating:

Choose a *variety* of foods every day
Emphasize cereals, breads, whole grain products, vegetables and fruit
Choose fat-free or low-fat dairy or milk products, foods prepared with little or no fat, low in saturated fats, trans fats, cholesterol
leaner meats, poultry, fish, beans, eggs and nuts
Limit salt (sodium), alcohol, caffeine and added sugars

Vegetarians *do* eat a variety of foods every day to obtain a balanced diet. Here's what a vegetarian diet provides:

6-11 Servings of whole grain bread, cereal, pasta and rice, oats & grains

1 serving = 1 slice of bread, 1 oz breakfast cereal. These food items are CARBOHYDRATES and should make up ½ your daily calorie intake and are the most important source of food energy in the world (energy is also provided by protein and fat). Carbohydrates are not present in animal foods. Countries which eat the most carbohydrates in their diets (such as starchy root vegetables and rice) have the lowest rates of obesity and chronic disease.

3-5 Servings of Vegetables

1 serving =1/2 cup vegetables, or 1 cup salad. These food items contain CARBOHYDRATES and VITAMINS & MINERALS and also contain

ANTIOXIDANTS which fight cancer and other diseases that compromise the immune system

2-4 Servings of Fruits

1 serving = 1 medium apple or ¾ cup fruit juice

2-3 Servings low-fat or non-fat milk, yogurt, fresh cheese and fortified alternatives (soy milk)

1 serving = ½ cup soymilk, or ½ cup calcium fortified orange juice
These food items contain CALCIUM and PROTEIN

2-3 servings Legumes, nuts, seeds and meat alternatives

1 serving = 1 veggie burger or 3 tab peanut butter
Legumes are beans, peas and lentils. Meat alternatives are Soy products including tofu and TVP (textured vegetable protein), which is made from the flakes that remain after oil is extracted from soybeans
Some meat alternatives are processed (like veggie burgers) and can be high in fat and salt, so use occasionally

Vegetable Fats & Oils, sweets and salt

Use these items "sparingly"

Many vegetarians also add omega-3 fatty acids, Vitamin B12 and Vitamin D to their daily intake

The Protein Myth

The number one concern for anyone considering a vegetarian diet is Protein. It shouldn't be such a concern. Let's look at the facts:

The average adult male protein requirement is 63 grams per day (RDA), and the average adult female is 50 grams per day. If you ate 1 cup of Tofu in a day, that's 40 grams of protein, compared to a 6 oz. steak which is already 42 grams of protein.

You could get half your entire daily requirement of protein just from eating breakfast!

1 cup of oatmeal 6 grams
1 cup whole or skim milk 8 grams
1 oz each sunflower seeds & flaxseeds 12 grams
2 slices of whole wheat toast 5 grams
Total: 31 grams!

Animal proteins are called complete proteins because they usually contain all 20 amino acids (9 of which are "essential," meaning our bodies don't produce them, we must get them from our food). Did you know that all amino acids in animal protein is derived from plants? The animals that we eat are vegetarians. All the essential amino acids can be found in plants, but not all plants have all the essentials. So vegetarians combine their proteins throughout the day to get all the essential amino acids. Protein is available in both animal and plant foods as well as low-fat dairy, eggs, nuts, and seeds.

Some protein is used for energy. But the body only uses what it needs, the rest is stored.

Iron

The iron provided in meat is more easily absorbed by the body but you can still get enough by eating iron rich plant foods such as legumes, spinach, Swiss chard, beet greens, black-strap molasses, bulgur, prune juice and prunes and dried fruits. Many breakfast cereal and juices are now fortified with iron. Drinking Vitamin C (orange juice) helps in the absorption of iron.

Calcium

We need about 800 milligrams a day (4 oz extra-firm tofu made with calcium salts contains 258 mg, 1 cup cooked collard greens 357 mg).
Low-fat dairy, collards, mustard greens and kale, broccoli, bok choy (one of my personal favorites), acorn squash and calcium fortified soymilk products (including tofu) all provide calcium. However, be careful how much calcium you get from dairy products because dairy products contain a lot of protein, the protein makes the kidneys work harder which in turn depletes the supply of calcium.
To boost calcium absorption, combine with Vitamin D.

Vitamin B-12

Dairy and eggs contain Vitamin B-12 as well as some "fortified" cereals (read the label on the box to see if B-12 has been added), B12 fortified soy or rice milk and cranberries.
Another great source of B12 is Marmite. Marmite is a dark brown spread which is usually put on toast but it is a great addition to spaghetti sauce as well as soup stock. It also contains riboflavin and niacin. A little goes a long way, so use it sparingly.

Folic Acid

Folic Acid works with B12 to form new cells, particularly in bone marrow. Good sources include wheat germ, peanuts, spinach, broccoli, cabbage, avocadoes, yeast extract, beans, peas, legumes.

Vitamin D

Found in dairy products and the sun—ultra violet rays from sunlight trigger vitamin D synthesis in the skin, creating vitamin D for our bodies to use. People living in Northern latitudes are at risk of insufficient vitamin D intake due to the lack of sunlight in winter months.

Zinc

Zinc is found in whole grain products, tofu, lentils, nuts, seeds, wheat germ and dairy. Our bodies absorb less zinc from plants because the fiber in some of these foods combines with the zinc and prevents full absorption. Look for meat substitutes that are zinc-fortified (such as deli slices).

Fat

The healthiest diet should contain 10-25% fat calories in the overall diet. There are 3 types of fat:

Saturated—from animal foods, whole milk, butter, hard cheeses and some nuts. Animal foods contain cholesterol because all animals have livers and the liver makes cholesterol (just as it does in your own body). Excess cholesterol is stored as plaque in your arteries.

There are two types of cholesterol—"bad" cholesterol is LDL (Low density Lipoproteins) and "good" cholesterol HDL (High density Lipoproteins)

You get far greater health benefits from using salad dressings made of extra virgin olive oil, fresh lemon juice, garlic and herbs, than from fat-free, water-based dressings from the supermarket.

Olives and olive oil (as well as most nuts and nut oils), increase HDL levels in the body.

Most oils are damaged when you cook with them at high heat, and produce toxic products. Choose sunflower, safflower, canola and peanut oil.

Polyunsaturated—has been shown to reduce the risk of heart disease.

Monounsaturated—has been shown to lower LDL cholesterol.

Trans Fat (also known as partially hydrogenated fat) is bad because it raises LDL levels and lowers beneficial HDL levels. Trans Fats are produced during the process of hydrogenation (turning a liquid into a solid as in the case of margarine). Watch for trans fat in hydrogenated vegetable oils, processed and fast foods.

Fiber

USDA recommends we eat 25 to 30 grams of fiber a day—no problem for a vegetarian!
Fiber is only available from plant foods. There are two types to do two different functions. "Water Soluble" and "Water Insoluble." Soluble is found in pectin, gums, and mucilage found in fruits and vegetables, legumes and oat brain. Insoluble is found in peels of fruits and vegetables, husks of whole grains.
Fiber helps move food through the gastro-intestinal track. It helps you feel full so you eat less. Soluble fiber can reduce your cholesterol level as it will bind to cholesterol and leave the body.

10 Tips for Healthy Eating

Buy fresh vegetables & fruit weekly
Avoid buying junk food
Avoid eating "fast food"
Avoid buying "processed" foods[3]
Include raw vegetables in your diet every day
Eat at least one "meatless" meal a week
Eat whole grain cereal and bread
Drink clean water, avoid soft drinks
Don't skip meals (eating regularly helps keep your blood sugar level constant)
Read the labels—Be an informed consumer

The Vegetarian Pantry

To make the recipes in this book, you may need to buy a few ingredients to have on hand:

Salt

For cooking, use Iodized salt, but when the taste matters, use sea salt and keep it in a salt grinder. I'm sure you'll notice a difference in taste.

Pepper

Buy peppercorns and use a pepper grinder so your pepper is always freshly ground.

Oils

There are lots of varieties to choose from but basically for salad dressings use olive oil (extra virgin, the best quality you can afford). Walnut oil is also nice in salad dressing. For cooking use vegetable oil. Look for canola, safflower or sunflower. For high heat stir-frying, peanut oil works well. You will also need sesame oil for some of the Asian sauces.

Vinegars

You will need wine vinegar: white wine, tarragon wine, red wine, and rice wine. Buy the best quality balsamic vinegar you can afford.

Seasonings

Buy small quantities of fresh herbs and spices. They lose a lot of their flavor if stored too long. Buy from a bulk food store or natural food store where the turnover of stock is constant.

Chili—powder, flakes and whole dried chilies
Cinnamon—powder
Cloves—powder
Cocoa—powder
Coriander—whole seeds
Curry—powder—try both Indian and East Indian; each has a unique taste
Cumin—whole seed
Fennel—whole seeds
Garlic—powder
Nutmeg—whole seed
Paprika—powder
Turmeric—powder

Tip: Dry roast seeds (such as coriander and cumin) in a non-stick fry pan over med-high heat just until they begin to "pop." Remove from heat and let cool before grinding. Dry roasting seeds greatly enhanced their flavor.

Fresh Herbs

When you get your bunch of herbs home, snip the stems a little with scissors and place the herbs in a tall glass. Put enough cold water in the glass to cover the stems. Cover the herbs with the clear plastic bag they came in and place in the fridge. You now have a "mini greenhouse" which will keep basil, parsley, coriander, mint, and dill fresh anywhere from a few days, up to a week. "Woody" herbs such as rosemary and thyme can be frozen. They will be easier to cut if you snip them with scissors the minute you take them out of the freezer.

Tip: before using fresh herbs, remove preliminary dirt from the leaves by running under cold water. Then fill a large bowl with cold water and dunk the herbs in the cold water a few times. Let them float in the water for 5-10 minutes and the rest of the dirt will fall off.

Hot Peppers

Be careful with these things! Always wear disposable latex or plastic gloves when preparing hot peppers (you can find disposable gloves at your local pharmacy). I keep fresh hot peppers in the freezer in small freezer bags. When ready to use, cut with a sharp knife while still frozen.

Hot peppers such as Jalapenos and Habaneras will be less hot if you don't use the seeds.

Try different varieties of peppers; they are not all the same level of heat. If you buy a pepper that you are not familiar with, use a very small quantity so that you don't ruin your dish by making it too hot; you can always add more heat but you can't take it away so easily.

I always keep a jar of pickled hot banana pepper rings and a jar of pickled jalapenos on hand for some recipes.

Mustards

You will need Prepared Mustard and Dijon. You can also buy grainy style Dijon for more texture and a slightly different taste.

Buy a small container of mustard powder (or a few tablespoons from the bulk food store).

Nuts

Peanuts (whole roasted and unsalted—I've included them here although not technically a nut), almonds, cashews, pecans, walnuts, pine nuts. Buy small quantities and keep in small plastic bags in your vegetable crisper in the fridge. Always taste nuts before using them to make sure they haven't become rancid.

Condiments

Asian Sauces:
Wasabe (either powder or paste in a tube)
Chili Garlic sauce

Hoisin sauce
Oyster sauce
Black Bean sauce

Soy Sauce I like two types: the conventional dark soy sauce which can be used for stir fry cooking and the lighter Tamari soy sauce which is very flavorful when making oriental sauces, dips and dressings

Fish Sauce—strict vegetarians look for artificial fish sauce. I often substitute Marmite[5]

Sesame Paste (also known as Tahini)

Indian Sauces

Most supermarkets now carry a selection of Indian sauces, which are ready to use. You just prepare your vegetables and/or legumes and when they are just about cooked, pour on the sauce and stir in. Heat and serve.

Canned Goods

Sun dried Tomatoes—I prefer those packed in oil, as they are ready to use. Just make sure you remove all the oil from them by patting them with a paper towel. They are also available dried. To use, soak them in boiling water for approx. 10-15 minutes until they re-hydrate.

Vegetable stock—you can buy vegetarian vegetable stock cubes. To "boost" the flavor, you can add sliced carrots and celery to the simmering stock. When making oriental soups, I often soak dried shitake mushrooms in hot water (about two tablespoons of mushrooms in ½ cup hot water) for about 20 minutes. Drain the water and add it to your vegetable stock.

Canned legumes (such as chick peas, lentils, kidney beans, turtle beans, pinto etc).

Tomatoes—whole, diced and ground (Plain or Italian style), tomato sauce and tomato paste

Corn (baby or miniature)

Artichokes—whole or pieces. I buy pieces in oil when I want to use them in a salad because they are more flavorful than canned

Rice

There is no need to buy "Instant" rice. Rice is very easy to make, and it cooks in about 15-20 minutes. When your meal will include rice, just remember to prepare the rice *first*. By the time you prepare your meal, the rice will be ready

My favorite rice is Basmati, which is from India. I also like Jasmine rice which is from Thailand and it is light and smells nice when cooking. Both of these rices are "long grain."

Short grain rice (such as Arborio) are used when making Risotto or Sushi. Short grain rice contains more starch so the rice will be stickier.

I sometimes buy a small quantity of wild rice to mix in with regular rice. It takes longer to cook, so prepare it separately.

Brown rice is unmilled or partly milled rice. It is very nutritious so you should give it a try.

Bulgar (also called Bulghur)—is a processed form of whole wheat and is more nutritious than rice. It is available from the bulk or natural food store. You're going to use it for *Falafel* and *Tabouli*, both Middle Eastern dishes.

Pasta and Noodles

Pasta

Buy whatever pasta noodles you like. The shapes are designed to hold different types of sauces. If you live near a fresh Italian pasta shop, fresh pasta cooks very quickly (usually in a few minutes).

Add salt to the water the pasta will be cooked in but don't add any oil. Oil will adhere to the cooked pasta and your sauce won't stay on the pasta. You can also add a little of the pasta cooking water to your finished sauce. The starch from the pasta will help thicken your sauce.

Noodles

Asian noodles don't take long to cook—just follow the package directions. Rinse in cold water and drain in a colander when cooked so they don't stick together.

In the Fridge

Butter and margarine—look for fat-reduced butter and margarine which is low in saturated fat, has non trans fat and is non-hydrogenated

Cheese—look for low-fat feta, cream cheese, and cheddar. Buy a piece of Parmesan cheese to grate it as you need it

Eggs—buy organic, free range

Cream—5% butter fat is usually sufficient for sauces unless something heavier is stated in the recipe

Yogurt—plain (low fat if you prefer)

Onions—I only cook with mild onions (Spanish or Vidali sweet onions). I keep onions on my counter in a basket until I need them. Once sliced open, I put left over onion into a plastic bag and store it in the crisper section of the fridge

If onions make you "cry," here's a good tip: before using, put them into the freezer for 10 minutes, then prepare as usual.

Garlic—buy fresh whole bulbs. If you don't use garlic very often, you can store peeled whole cloves in the fridge in a small bottle filled with vodka.

Tofu—(see the 'Introduction to Tofu' section). Buy a block, which is sealed in a shrink-wrapped package or in water. If you have any leftover tofu, transfer it to a plastic container with a tight fitting lid. Cover with cold water and keep refrigerated. Use within four or five days (changing the water daily will help keep it fresh).

Tools of the Trade

Having the right equipment on hand makes preparing any kind of meal a lot easier. These tools will help you to make quick, delicious vegetarian meals:

Knives

You should have a good quality Chef's knife. Choose a size that you are comfortable handling. You will get frustrated pretty quickly if your knife is not kept sharp. Buy yourself a knife sharpener or hone so that you can quickly get your blade back up to speed.

Have an assortment of small cutting and paring knives to prepare and peel small vegetables.

I also use a small Asian cleaver for slicing vegetables but you could use your Chef's knife.

Citrus Reamer

This is a small tool with a pointed ridged centre. Basically, you cut your citrus in half and place one half on top of the reamer. You then turn the fruit so that it grinds against the ridges. This helps to extract most of the liquid.

Peeler

Use a vegetable peeler instead of trying to peel vegetables with a knife. You will loose less vegetable. The peel often contains higher concentrations of pesticides than the fruit or vegetable. The peel can also contain harmful bacteria. For these reasons, peel as many fruits and vegetables as you can. If you are using the peel, always wash it first.

Garlic Press

When you want the garlic to be fully integrated into a sauce, use a press. Read the recipes carefully; finely chopped garlic will be less potent in flavor than pressed garlic, which releases the garlic juices.

Sieve

This is a large, flat round spoon-shaped tool that has small holes in it. It's great for stir-frying or lifting vegetables out of water.

Tongs

This is my favorite all-purpose kitchen tool. Keep several sizes on hand at all times. You can stir with them, pick things up and toss a salad. Long handled tongs can help you avoid getting burned if you're reaching for something across a burner, using hot oil or trying to turn food which is in the oven.

Graters

Try to purchase a variety of graters for different purposes. You will need a small, fine grater for nutmeg, ginger and garlic. A "Micro Plane" grater is good for hard cheese (such as Parmesan) and a box grater can be used for regular cheese (such as cheddar) and some vegetables (such as carrots).

Whisks

My stirring and mixing ability improved drastically when I started using whisks. A small whisk can help you perfect homemade salad dressing, a large whisk works beautifully when mixing flour and other dry ingredients together.

Scissors

You will find a million uses for a good pair of kitchen scissors. You can not only use them to open packages, but to chop herbs, trim your pie crust, snip green bean ends, chop canned tomatoes into smaller pieces…the list will grow as you start to look at scissors as another invaluable kitchen tool.

Equipment

Sauté Pans

I use non-stick sauté pans as much as possible. A small pan is useful for toasting spices and sautéing a small quantity of onions, and a large pan (10-12" diameter) is good for just about everything else.

Your food won't stick and cleaning non-stick pans will be much quicker and easier. A few words of advice: *never* use metal tools on non-stick pots or pans; it will damage the non-stick surface. I usually use wooden spoons or wooden scrapers. Wash your non-stick cookware separately from other tools so that it doesn't get scratched and store your pans with a pad between them so they don't get scraped. I usually use old oven mitts or pot holders for this purpose.

Avoid over heating your non-stick pans when empty. Do not allow them to get "smoking" hot.

Wok

(See section on 'Stir Frying'). If you don't want to use a Wok, a large sauté pan will work but you may have a little trouble keeping your ingredients from jumping out of the pan when you're stir-frying.

Look for a non-stick Wok or the traditional uncoated carbon steel.

Sauce Pans

Here again, my favorites are non-stick. I have a small one for cooking rice and a larger one for sauces.

Colanders

You will need a large, bowl shaped metal or plastic colander for draining pasta and a fine colander (or sieve) for washing rice.

Mixing Bowls

You should have a variety of sizes on hand: small, medium and at least a couple of large size. I prefer stainless steel but glass or ceramic is also a good choice, although the bowls will be heavier to maneuver.

Salad Spinner

This is optional but will save you a lot of time if you make a lot of salads (which I hope you do!). The salad greens can be washed right in the spinner and then "spun dry" afterwards.

If you don't have a spinner, wash your greens then lay them out on clean dish towels. Roll the dish towels up to absorb excess water. You can also use paper towel instead of cloth towels.

Spice Grinder

I bought a coffee grinder that I use just for spices (I have a separate grinder for coffee). You can use a mortar and pestle (this is a little bowl with a special pounding stick) but I find the grinder does a quicker, more even job.

Food Processor

This is a great piece of equipment, which will really speed things up for you in the kitchen. It will grind and mix ingredients faster (and more uniformly) than you can do by hand. A few words of advice: as soon as you're finished using your food processor, rinse all the components under hot, running water (even if you will be using it again later) as the parts can be hard to clean once the processed food has dried on them.

Introduction to Legumes
(Beans, Peas and Lentils)

Legumes (or Beans), form an integral part of the vegetarian diet. Beans and rice when served together offer the vegetarian a complete protein; therefore the protein requirement can be met in a single meal.

Most of the legume recipes I've chosen call for canned beans. I use canned for simplicity sake. I can quickly prepare a meal using canned beans anytime I want. I often make dishes with two or more kinds of beans, for variety of taste and texture. In this case, I use about ½ can of each type, and freeze the rest. Beans freeze beautifully in their own liquid. Allow the container to de-frost, and rinse in a colander.

Dried beans are a little tastier and have more texture so use them when you have the time. With the exception of lentils, most require soaking overnight so you have to factor that into your meal preparation.

Your natural food store or neighborhood ethnic store will usually have a variety of dried beans on hand. Try all of them, even if you don't recognize some of the names. Most are really tasty and interesting.

Beans are the vegetarian's secret weapon. In the lowly bean, we find the best source of vegetable protein and great fiber.

I know what you're thinking—they cause gas. Actually, when eaten regularly, they don't cause gas because your digestive system gets used to them. You can also put a product called "Beano" on the beans prior to eating and that will help. Adzuki beans will cause less gas the Navy beans (the kind usually used for Baked Beans).

If you plan to use dried beans, replacing the soaking water and cooking water regularly throughout the preparation process may also reduce flatulence.

If you can remember to soak the beans the day before you plan to use them, I recommend dried—the flavor is superior to canned. Here are two soaking methods:

Regular soak—soak 1 cup of dried beans in 3 cups of cold water. Leave overnight or at least 6 hours. (Change the water a couple of times if you can remember).

Quick soak—Put the beans and water in a saucepan and boil for 3 minutes. Remove from heat and let stand for 1 hour. The boiling cracks the skin of the beans so they will cook faster.

Many of the bean recipes can be made with a variety of beans. I encourage you to try as many bean varieties as you can find and make note of your favorites.

Peas

Chick peas (also known as Garbanzo beans), are high in dietary fiber, zinc and protein (1/2 cup contains 17 gr fiber and 19 gr of protein). They are also a good source of carbohydrates and are suitable for the diabetic diet.

Green Peas (also known as Matar Dal) and yellow peas (Yellow Matar Dal) are split and don't require any soaking.

Lentils

Lentils all cook quickly, and don't need soaking. Red lentils cook the fastest.

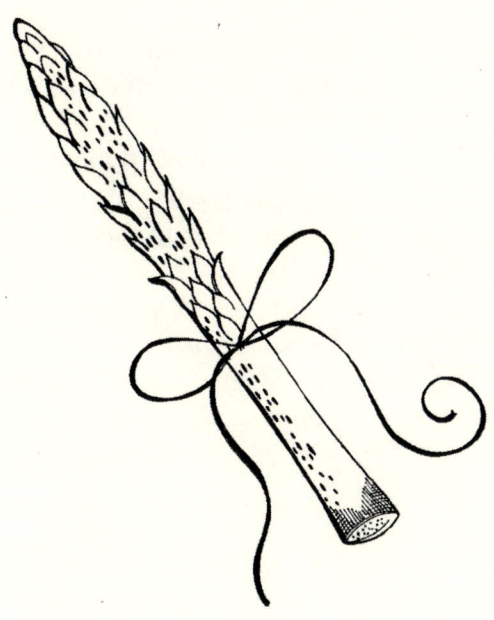

Did you know that peanuts are not nuts but are legumes? 100 grams (approx. 3.5 oz) of peanuts contain 27 grams of protein!

Introduction to Grains

Grains are barley, wheat bran, wheat germ, bulgur and cracked wheat, brown rice and white rice, buckwheat, cornmeal and hominy, oats, quinoa, and wild rice.

There are a lot of grains out there that are not featured in this book. I urge you to try them all in recipes to see which ones you like. Don't be afraid to substitute one grain for another in this book's recipes. If you really like a particular grain, use it!

Grains are rich in complex carbohydrates, vitamins, minerals and fiber. For example, rice is a good source of thiamine, riboflavin and niacin. Rice provides 20 percent of the world's dietary energy supply, which makes it the most consumed cereal grain and the world's largest crop!

How to cook White Rice

We eat a lot of rice at our house. My favorites are Basmati (a long grain Indian variety) and Fragrant Thai Jasmine rice (also long grain). Long grain rice is the most common cultivated and used rice in the U.S. Long grain rice cooks up fluffy and doesn't stick together.

Short grain rice (such as Italian Arborio), is very starchy, and tends to stick together. For this reason, it is suitable for Sushi and Risotto.

Many people think that cooking rice from "scratch" is difficult and time consuming—Nothing could be farther from the truth!

When your meal will include rice, just remember to put the rice on to cook first—I guarantee by the time your main dish is ready, your rice will be ready too.

Put the rice in a small sieve or colander. Rinse under cold running water, until the water runs clear. You can also rest the colander in a bowl of cold water as you run water over it; this way you will see when the water runs clear. Drain.

Use one cup of rice to 2 cups of water. Add a pinch of salt to the cooking water.

Bring the water to a boil in a *non-stick* sauce pan (a 1 Litre/1 quart saucepan is fine for this quantity of rice; use a 1.5 Litre/2 quart saucepan for larger quantities). Slowly add the washed rice.

Give it a quick stir. Cover and reduce the heat to simmer.

DO NOT REMOVE THE LID TO CHECK THE RICE! (Choose a saucepan with a glass lid so you can watch the rice cooking without being tempted to lift the lid). The rice should be done in 15 to 20 minutes (depending on the age of the rice, type of rice and your stove). The first time you cook a different type of rice, check it after 15 minutes—it should look "fluffy," all the water should be absorbed and it should be tender to the taste.

"Fluff" the rice with a fork (or wooden spoon if your saucepan is non-stick). Put the lid back on and remove the pot from the heat. Let sit 5 minutes and serve. You can also leave the rice covered in the saucepan until the rest of the meal is ready; no need to re-heat.

Leftover rice is great for making fried rice. Leftover rice can be frozen. Just remove the lid, and put the frozen rice in its microwaveable container in the microwave. Cover both the container and a small bowl of water with a sheet of plastic wrap (leave a small opening to allow steam to escape). Microwave on "defrost" power for approx. 5-10 minutes (checking after 5 minutes, then every couple of minutes), until the rice is defrosted and heated completely. The addition of the bowl of water will keep the rice from drying out.

A word about Wheat Germ

Wheat Germ is one of the most nutritional products available, containing 23 nutrients (including more potassium and iron than any other food source). Wheat germ contains approximately 28% protein (more than most meat products). You can find wheat germ in whole wheat bread and whole grain breakfast cereals. Wheat germ can be purchased at the natural foods store. Just sprinkle it on your morning cereal or yoghurt or add it to vegetable dishes—what an easy way to get a nutrition "boost."

Did you know that wild rice is actually *seeds*? They are the seeds from a group of grasses which grow in the shallow waters of small lakes and slow-flowing streams.

Introduction to Nuts & Seeds

Nuts

You can improve the texture and flavor of just about any dish by adding nuts or seeds. Nuts (such as walnuts and almonds), are thought to lower blood cholesterol levels. Cashews, which contain vitamin E and selenium, have been linked to a reduced risk of certain cancers.

Nuts (such as pine nuts) add protein to any meal. Cashews and Peanuts go well with Asian and Indian dishes as well as cooked vegetables. They should be chopped up and sprinkled on just before serving.

Seeds

I like to use sunflower seeds and pumpkin seeds interchangeably in pasta recipes and salads. Tiny, delicious sesame seeds can be added to Asian dishes whenever you want.

Legumes and Grains: Legume Recipes

Bean Burritos

This is a very simple, nutritious Mexican style meal. Serve with Avocado* and fresh salsa on the side. Watch the amount of Jalapeños, chili powder and Tabasco you use if you're serving this to people who don't like their food too spicy.

Serving option: Instead of tortillas, spoon bean mixture directly onto a plate, sprinkle with cheddar and drizzle with a large spoonful of tomato sauce. Microwave as directed. When heated, dot surface with tortilla chips and serve.

15 minutes preparation (including 5 min preparation time for the avocado)

1 ½ min each serving on High in microwave

Drizzle a large non-stick sauté pan with 1 or tab of oil. Sauté onions until golden brown (about five minutes medium-high heat). Add garlic and sauté one minute more.

Transfer refried beans to a medium bowl. Add sautéed onion mixture and jalapenos. Stir to combine.

In a small bowl, combine tomato sauce with BBQ sauce, chili powder and Tabasco. Taste before serving. Add more seasonings if sauce isn't spicy enough for you. If its too spicy, add a little more tomato sauce to dilute.

Divide refried bean mixture evenly between 6 to 8 tortillas**Spoon mixture down the centre of each tortilla. Top each mixture with grated cheddar. Roll up. Place on microwaveable plate, with the tortilla seam facing down. Spoon tomato sauce evenly over tortillas. Cover plate with plastic wrap (leaving a small opening along one edge for steam to escape). Microwave on high for 1 or 1 ½ minutes until hot and cheese has melted.

Remove plastic wrap and garnish each tortilla with a little cilantro. Serve with a helping of fresh salsa and avocado on the side.

* Avocado—in a medium bowl, chop 2 ripe avocadoes into bite-size pieces. Add 1 medium clove of very finely minced garlic, juice of ¼ fresh lemon and salt and pepper to taste. Mix with a fork just to combine.
** If you use small tortillas you will be able to fill more. I usually buy medium size tortillas. This recipe will fill 8 medium torillas.

Vegetable oil for the pan
1 can refried beans
½ large sweet onion, finely diced
1 large clove garlic, finely minced
1 or 2 tab pickled jalapeños, diced
1 ½ cup mild or medium cheddar, grated
¾ can tomato sauce
1 or 2 tab hickory flavor BBQ sauce
1 tab (or more)chili powder
generous shake chipotle Tabasco sauce to taste
Package of fresh, soft tortillas, any size
Fresh coriander leaves, chopped for garnish

Bean Burgers

These burgers are nice because they have texture. You can try mixing them in your food processor but just process the mixture enough so it holds together; you don't want the mixture to turn into mush.

Serve them alone on a plate with a vegetable side dish or serve them with "hamburger fixins" and homemade fries.

10 minutes preparation
10 minutes frying
makes about 8 patties*

Put all ingredients (except oil) into a large bowl and mash with a potato masher until combined (or briefly process in a food processor).

Scoop enough mixture into your hand to make a patty about ¼" thick and about 3" round.

Drizzle a large non-stick sauté pan with enough oil to coat the pan. Place on medium-high heat. When oil is heated, add 3 or 4 patties to the pan. Fry until the bottom is golden brown, about 3-5 minutes. Using a spatula, gently lift each patty and turn it over to fry the other side. When both sides are fried, carefully remove from heat and drain on paper towels.

Serve on hamburger buns with lettuce, tomato etc. These are very good topped with a little corn relish or salsa.

* If you prefer to serve them in a pita pocket, make each patty slightly smaller (about 2" diameter). Mixture will make about 10-12 patties this size.

1-2 tab vegetable oil for the pan
1 ½ cups canned beans such as Pinto or Romano
1 ½ cups Italian bread crumbs
1 egg
¼ cup bran
¼ cup sesame seeds
½ medium sweet onion, chopped
1 clove garlic, pressed
2 tab fresh parsley
1 heaping tab onion soup mix
¼ cup soy sauce
¼ cup cider vinegar
1 teas ground cumin

Bean Chili

I usually recommend canned beans to save time. If you have a crock pot lying around somewhere, try this recipe. Dried beans DO impart a richer texture to legume recipes, so give this one a try one weekend when you have all day to wait for the crock pot to work its "magic."

Preparation time: 10 minutes
Cooking time: 6-8 hours in crock pot set on High

Soak kidney beans overnight in 5 cups cold water. Discard any "floaters" (beans that float to the top of the water) and drain.

Sauté onions and garlic in oil five minutes. Add carrot and celery, sauté another 5 minutes until tender. Add mushrooms and brown slightly.

Transfer mixture to crock pot. Add beans and remaining ingredients including 3 cups of water. Stir. Cover and cook all day or overnight.

Tip: you can substitute other types of beans: use red and white kidney beans, or red kidney and navy, kidney and Romano, kidney and black beans. Refer to bean package for individual soaking directions.

1 cup dried kidney beans
1 cup dried green lentils
8 cups water
1 ½ cups sweet onions, chopped
3 cloves pressed garlic
1/3 cup each diced carrot, celery
3 cups fresh mushrooms, diced

LAUREEN OSBORNE

¼ cup vegetable oil
5 tab chili powder
1 tab dried oregano
2 teas ground coriander, cumin
2 tab paprika (sweet, mild)
1 whole dried chili, crushed or ½ teas red pepper flakes (or to taste)
1 19 oz can whole tomatoes (chopped) including liquid
1/3 cup soy sauce
salt & pepper to taste

Bean & Cheese Quesadillas

You want to chop the ingredients finely so that they get the opportunity to cook in the brief amount of time they spend grilling.

Prepare your side dishes before you start so that the quesadillas can be served while they are still warm.

10 minutes preparation
20 minutes cooking
Serves 4

Finely chop all ingredients. Grate cheese.

Lay out four tortillas and divide mixture evenly between all four tortillas. Place a second tortilla on top of each one.

Carefully transfer one quesadilla to a large pre-heated non-stick sauté pan that has been drizzled with vegetable oil. Heat should be set at medium-high.

Immediately pat the surface of the tortilla so that the cheese has a chance to melt and hold the whole thing together. After a few minutes, lift one edge of the quesadilla to see how it looks. The bottom should be browning, but not burning. When the bottom is browned to your liking, carefully turn the quesadilla over using a large non-stick spatula. Carefully grill the second side.

Transfer to individual plates. Cut into wedges like a pie.

Serve with homemade salsa and guacamole or salad.

For a crispier quesadilla, use a little more oil.

1 cup Mexican Style Bean Salad*
1 tomato, seeded and finely chopped
1 pickled jalapeño, finely chopped
1 clove garlic, minced
½ cup cilantro, finely chopped
2 tab green onions, finely chopped
1 ½ cup medium cheddar cheese, grated
8 medium flour tortillas
vegetable oil for the pan

*Look for canned mixed beans in your grocery store

Bean & Rice Burgers

Legumes combined with rice form a complete protein. This means you are getting your full protein requirement by eating one or two of these "burgers."

For an Italian flavor, serve them with the sauce.

I like to substitute cheddar for mozzarella because mozzarella can be a little gooey.

20 minute preparation
30 minutes baking at 350^0
6 servings

Cook onions and garlic in oil until softened. Add zucchini, mushrooms, thyme, cumin, soy sauce and Worcestershire. Cook an additional 3-5 minutes.

Transfer to food processor. Add beans and rice, and cornstarch. Season with salt & pepper. Pulse a few times until blended (do not over pulse so you still have some texture).

Transfer mixture to a bowl. Blend in egg whites with a fork. Cover the bowl and refrigerate ½ hour or longer until the mixture firms up. Spoon enough mixture from the bowl to form a pattie. Form mixture into 6 patties. Coat each pattie with breadcrumbs on both sides (to coat each pattie, pour the breadcrumbs into a re-sealable baggie, then add a pattie, and shake *gently* to coat on both sides. Carefully remove from baggie).

Add a little oil to coat the bottom of a large sauté pan. Place on medium heat. Carefully add patties and brown on both sides (about 2 minutes per side). Transfer browned patties to a baking sheet and bake in the oven 30 minutes.

Meanwhile combine tomato sauce and seasonings. Warm mixture in a small saucepan.

When patties are baked, remove from baking sheet and place one or two on an oven-proof serving plate. Pour a little sauce over each pattie and sprinkle with grated cheeses. Put under the oven broiler for a few minutes until cheese melts and starts to bubble (keep an eye on it so the cheese doesn't burn).

Tip: You could use the microwave instead of the broiler—cover each prepared plate with a sheet of plastic wrap (leave a small opening for the steam to escape), and microwave for 1 or 2 minutes until the cheese melts.

2 tab vegetable or olive oil
1 small onion, finely diced
1 large clove garlic, finely diced
¼ lb mushrooms, finely diced
½ small zucchini, grated
1 tsp each thyme, ground cumin
1 tab soy sauce
½ tab Worcestershire sauce
2 cups canned Romano or White Kidney beans (or a combination of both)
1 cup cooked white rice
2 tab cornstarch
2 egg whites
¼ cup Italian breadcrumbs

Sauce (optional):
1 14 oz can Italian tomato sauce
1 teas oregano

¼ teas red pepper flakes
½ cup shredded mozzarella or mild cheddar
½ cup grated fresh Parmesan
salt & pepper to taste

Beans in Tomato Sauce

This tastes similar to Chili but is faster to make.

15 preparation
15 minutes cooking
4 servings

Sauté celery, onion, peppers and garlic in a large sauté pan in oil until vegetables are tender (5-8 min). Add beans, tomatoes (and their juice), tomato paste, lemon juice and spices. Stir to combine. Taste the mixture and add salt and pepper as desired. Add a dash of Tabasco if desired. Cover and simmer for approx. 15 minutes until tomatoes start to break down and form a sauce.

Serve with plain white rice or toast.

Optional: sprinkle each serving with finely chopped coriander or parsley, or sprinkle each serving with grated cheddar .

1 or 2 tab oil for the pan
2 cans pinto beans, drained
1 ½ cups canned tomatoes, chopped (including the juice from the can)
½ cup chopped celery
¼ cup sweet pepper, chopped (red or green peppers or both)
½ cup chopped sweet onion
1 small can tomato paste
2 tab fresh lemon juice
1 teas ground cumin
½ teas red chili flakes

VEGETARIAN FOR A DAY

2 cloves garlic, pressed
salt & pepper to taste
dash Tabasco

Black Bean Biryani

This is a "One Dish Wonder" for those nights when you're looking for something a little more exotic. If you really want to go "over the top," serve this Biryani as a side dish with *Pineapple Meatballs*.

10 minutes preparation
25 minutes cooking
Serves 4 as a main course
Serves 6 as a side dish

Bring stock and pineapple juice to a boil in a medium non-stick saucepan. Add the rice. Reduce heat to low and cook covered, for 15 minutes. Do not remove the lid during cooking (check the rice for doneness *after* 15 minutes of cooking). When the rice is cooked, keep covered and remove from the heat.

In a medium, non-stick sauté pan, melt butter on medium heat. Add the spices and cook about one minute until the spices start to give an aroma. Add the garlic and sauté 30 seconds. Add the vegetables and black beans. Stir to combine. Sauté the mixture 5-7 minutes until the vegetables are cooked (carefully remove a piece of red pepper. Cool it under running cold water. Put it in your mouth and see if it is cooked to your liking. If it's not cooked enough, sauté the mixture a few minutes longer).

Put the cooked rice in a large bowl. Add sautéed vegetable/bean mixture to the rice. Add raisins and cashews and stir to thoroughly combine. Transfer to a nice serving dish and sprinkle with sliced green onion just before serving.

VEGETARIAN FOR A DAY

1 cup Basmati rice—well rinsed and drained
1 ½ cups vegetable stock
½ cup pineapple juice

3 tab butter
½ tab curry powder
¼ teas each ground tumeric, cumin, cardamom, cinnamon

1 clove garlic—finely diced
2" piece of sweet red pepper, finely diced
½ stalk of celery, finely diced
¼ can black beans, rinsed & drained

Optional:
¼ cup sultana raisins
¼ cup toasted cashews
2 sliced green onions

Black Beans & Rice

This recipe, with its combination of beans and rice, is a staple dish in many countries. It is a one dish meal.

10 minutes preparation
10 minutes cooking
6 servings

Add oil to a large sauté pan and heat on medium-high. Add onion and garlic and sauté until the onion starts to soften. Add celery and sweet pepper. Sauté another 2-3 minutes. Add canned tomatoes and seasonings. Stir in beans and rice. Season with salt and pepper. If using, add Worcestershire and hot sauce to taste. Cover and simmer 5-10 minutes until vegetables are tender.

Transfer to individual plates and sprinkle with cheese and chopped cilantro.

1 tab vegetable or olive oil
½ medium sweet onion, diced
2 cloves garlic, finely diced
1 stalk of celery, peeled and diced
½ sweet red or green pepper, diced
1 19 oz can Italian tomatoes, chopped
1 teas each chili powder, ground cumin
½ teas thyme
1 cup canned black beans, drained & rinsed
1 cup cooked rice
Salt and Pepper to taste

Optional:
A generous sprinkle Worcestershire sauce

Dash hot sauce (to taste)

Optional Garnish:
Grated cheddar
Chopped fresh cilantro

Chick Peas in Tahini Sauce

10 minutes preparation
20 minutes cooking
4 servings

Placed toasted spices and cardamom and turmeric in a spice grinder and grind until it becomes a powder. Heat the butter and oil in a large non-stick sauté pan on medium-low heat. Add the onions and sauté a couple of minutes.

Add the garlic and sauté an additional minute. Add all the ingredients from the grinder and salt. Stir to combine. Reduce heat slightly and leave to fry gently, stirring occasionally while you prepare the sauce an additional few minutes.

In your food processor or blender combine 6 tablespoons of the chick peas with all the liquid from the chick pea can, tahini and tomato paste. Process or blend until a sauce is formed.

Transfer the sauce to the sauté pan and add the remaining chick peas. Stir to combine. Cover and simmer gently (stirring occasionally) for 5-10 minutes until the flavors have combined.

Just before serving, sprinkle with lemon juice and add more salt (if necessary), to taste.

VEGETARIAN FOR A DAY

Toast:
1 tablespoon cumin seeds
1 tablespoon coriander seeds
½ teaspoon black peppercorns
1/8 teaspoon red chili flakes (optional)

1/8 teaspoon ground cardamom
1 teaspoon ground turmeric

1 tablespoon butter
1 tablespoon vegetable oil

½ large sweet onion, finely diced
3 large cloves garlic, finely minced
1/8 teaspoon salt

Sauce:
1 19 oz can chick peas, drained (save liquid)and remove any skins that are peeling
1 ½ tablespoons Tahini
4 tablespoons tomato paste (approximately ½ small can, 156 ml)
¼ lemon—juiced
salt to taste

Cucumber Raita

If you make an Indian meal, this is a nice side dish to have along in case things get too spicy for you. It also compliments the flavor of most Indian dishes and its very easy to make.

For a variation, you can add 1 tab finely diced sweet onion to the cucumber. You can also serve Raita plain with no cucumber.

5 minutes preparation

Just before serving, mix all ingredients together in a small bowl. Add more salt to taste, if necessary.

2 cups natural yoghurt
½ English cucumber, peeled, cut into small dice and drained*
½ teas salt
¼ teas black pepper
½ teas toasted cumin seeds, ground

* Place diced cucumber in a small colander and allow to drain for a few minutes if you have time. Too much liquid in the cucumber will make your raita watery (but some people prefer it that way).

Curried Chick Peas

These are a delicious introduction to Indian cooking. It is very easy to make. If you have the time, pop the chick peas out of their transparent shells the day before. Let them sit in the liquid from the can overnight and they will be even more delicious!

10 minute preparation
10 minute cooking
4 servings

Melt butter in large non-stick sauté pan. Add the curry powder, and stir one minute, Add onions, peppers, garlic, celery, thyme and tomato. Add 2 tab of liquid from the chick pea can. Simmer a few minutes. Add chick peas and the rest of the liquid from the can. Cover and simmer for approx. 10 minutes.

You can adjust the curry powder up or down depending on your taste. For more heat, add a few drops of hot sauce if you like.

1 19 oz can chick peas*, save liquid
2 teas butter
2 teas curry powder
1 small onion, finely chopped
3 cloves garlic, pressed
½ sweet pepper (red or green), finely chopped
½ stalk celery, finely chopped
1 small tomato, finely chopped
1 sprig fresh thyme

*chick peas are also known as Garbanzo beans.

Dahl

This dish is a staple of Indian cooking. Dahl is usually made with lentils or split peas. It can be thinned with vegetable stock to make a soup.

5 minute preparation
20 minutes cooking
4 servings

To make the curry powder, toast mustard, fennel, fenugreek, cumin and coriander seeds in a small non-stick frying pan. Toast over high heat until they begin to smoke or "pop" (it won't take more than a few minutes). Immediately stir and remove from heat. Do not burn them.

Grind the toasted seeds in a clean coffee or spice grinder for 30 seconds or until seeds become a powder. When ground, add turmeric, cardamom, chili and peppercorns. Grind again until the spice mixture is incorporated. You have now made a "curry powder."

Using a medium non-stick sauté pan, heat the butter and oil over medium-low heat. When heated, add onion and the curry powder. Fry gently for 15 minutes, stirring occasionally.

Meanwhile, pour the canned lentils and tomato juice into a large non-stick saucepan. Heat gently over medium-low heat. Season with a little salt to taste.

When the curry mixture is fried, remove from the heat. Divide the mixture in half and add half of the mixture to the pot of lentils. Stir in the lemon juice. Taste it and add more salt (and lemon juice) if desired. Return to the heat and cook for another 5 minutes.

Note: Use the other half of the curry mixture to make *"Curried Vegetables"*

Lentils:
1 19 oz can green lentils or other canned lentils
1 cup tomato juice or tomato cocktail juice
1 tab (or more) fresh lemon juice
salt to taste*

Curry Powder:
2 teas each: mustard seeds, fennel seeds, fenugreek
1 tab each cumin seeds, coriander seeds
2 teas ground turmeric
¼ teas cardamom seeds (about three pods remove seeds from pod)
1 dried hot red chili
1 teas whole black peppercorns
2 tab butter, 2 tab oil
1 cup finely diced onion

* Start with ½ teas of salt—you can always add more salt but its difficult to correct a dish that is "over-salted."

Falafel - Recipe #1

When I want an easy Friday night, watch a movie-kind-of meal, this is one I choose. Serve these sandwiches with fries and/or a salad.

10 minutes preparation
5-8 minutes frying
Makes about 20 patties

Put all the falafel ingredients into a food processor. If the mixture appears too dry to hold together, drizzle a little of the liquid from the canned chick peas through the processor's feeder. Add a couple of tablespoons at a time and process for 5-10 seconds. Check the mixture's consistency. As soon as the mixture is holding together, you've probably got enough moisture. Don't add too much liquid or the falafels will not fry properly.

Pour a couple of tabs of the olive oil into a large non-stick sauté pan. Heat over medium heat. When the oil is heated, take a spoonful of falafel mixture from the processor. Put the spoonful into your hands and form it into a patty about 2" diameter, and about the same thickness as a hamburger. Using a non-stick spatula, gently slide the falafel into the oil (being careful not to splash yourself with the hot oil). Form enough patties to fit comfortably in the pan. Fry the patties in the olive oil until golden brown. Carefully lift each patty and turn it over to fry the other side (frying will take 2 or 3 minutes per side). Using the spatula, carefully remove each falafel and drain it on paper towels.

Slice a pita in half and open each half to form a pocket*** Add the garnishes as desired. Insert one or two fried falafel on top of the garnishes. Spoon a little Falafel sauce over each.

*** Falafels can also be made into balls instead of patties. Remove a soup spoonful of mixture and using your hands, roll it into a ball about the size of a ping pong ball. Fry the balls on all sides by giving the pan a gentle shake every 30 seconds or so. Remove each ball and drain on paper towel.

Instead of cutting the pita in half, use a sharp knife, slice the pita in half *horizontally*. Place 3 or 4 balls along one edge of one slice of the pita. Garnish as desired and add the sauce. Turn the outside edge of the pita over to cover everything. After one roll, tuck the ends in about 1" so the ingredients don't fall out the ends. Continue rolling until the pita looks like a burrito.

Falafel ingredients:
6 cups canned chick peas (3 19 oz. cans), save the liquid from the cans
1 cup finely chopped parsley
½ cup fine bulgur
4 cloves garlic, minced
2 tab fresh lemon juice
Salt & pepper to taste
1 hot green chili
2 tab ground cumin
½ cup whole wheat flour
¼ cup olive oil

Garnish:
Shredded iceberg or romaine lettuce, tomato and onion slices, pickled turnip*
Pita bread—size small, white or whole wheat

Falafel Sauce:
2 teas Tahini**
1 cup plain natural yoghurt
2 small cloves garlic, pressed

Lemon juice (optional, to taste)

*These are sold in Middle Eastern grocery stores. They are a pink/purple color and come in jars either whole or in slices.

** Tahini is a brown paste, very similar to peanut butter but is made from ground sesame seeds. You can substitute peanut butter but the flavor won't be authentic.

Falafel - Recipe #2

For a little variety, try different kinds of beans every time you make these. One type of bean will quickly become your family's favorite. The addition of cumin and coriander gives these patties their middle-eastern flavor.

If you have a very large food processor, it won't be necessary to do two batches. Just add all the beans at the same time and process as directed.

10 minutes preparation
5 minutes processing
10 minutes frying

Add half the beans and all ingredients to your food processor. Process just until the beans are starting to mush (don't over process or the patties won't have any texture). Remove the mixture and place it in a large bowl. Add the rest of the beans to the processor along with a little of the liquid from the canned beans (add just enough liquid to process the beans—see the instructions given in Falafel Recipe #1).

Remove this mixture and add it to the bowl. Mix everything together. If the mixture is too dry, add 1 tab of liquid from the cans and mix in. Keep adding by tablespoon until the mixture has the right consistency: moist enough to form into patties but not wet.

Season to taste with salt, pepper and a little Tabasco sauce (optional), and mix well.

Using a large soup spoon, put the mixture into your hand. Form into a small patty about 2" diameter.

Pre-heat a large non-stick sauté pan with a drizzle of vegetable oil (enough to coat the entire bottom). Heat oil on medium-high. Add patties, leaving room between each one so you can flip them over. Fry for 3-4 minutes on each side. Drain on paper towels.

You can serve these patties on their own or "sandwich style" tucked into pita bread (see Falafel Recipe #1 for serving suggestions).

Falafel ingredients:
1 19 oz can beans—choose Pinto, Romano or Fava beans, rinsed and drained*
½ 19 oz can chick peas, rinsed and drained*
¼ sweet onion, finely diced
1 large clove garlic, finely chopped
2 green onions, finely chopped
¼ cup cilantro, finely chopped
1 teas salt
1 teas baking powder
1 teas each *toasted and ground* coriander seeds, and cumin

Vegetable oil for the pan

1 package small Pita bread (optional)

* Keep the drained liquid—you might need it to moisten the mixture when it is in the food processor.

Lentil Biryani

This is a complete meal because of the addition of lentils.

10 minutes preparation
30 minutes cooking

Heat the oil on medium-low in a large non-stick saucepan. Add the vegetables and garlic and sauté until softened, approx. 5 minutes. Add the Madras or curry sauce and stir to combine. Add the drained rice and stir with a wooden spoon to coat the rice completely. Carefully pour in the vegetable stock. Increase the heat to high and when it comes to a boil, reduce the heat to low and cover. Gently simmer for 15 minutes. Stir in the lentils and cilantro. Return to the heat and simmer for 5 minutes more or until the lentils are heated.

Remove from the heat and let stand covered, for 5 minutes longer and serve.

To serve, mound the Biryani on a platter which has been rimmed with alternating slices of tomato and cucumber.

1 ½ tab vegetable oil
2 tab Madras Cooking Sauce medium or hot or any other bottled madras sauce or curry sauce
2 cups vegetable stock
1 cup Basmati or regular long grain rice, rinsed and drained
1 stalk celery, peeled and finely diced
¼ peeled red onion, finely diced

2 large scallions (or green onions), outer layer and root removed, sliced in 3 sections lengthwise, then finely diced
2 tab fresh cilantro, chopped
1 large clove garlic, smashed and finely minced
½ 19 oz can lentils, drained

Garnish (Optional):
1 ripe tomato, sliced
½ small cucumber, peeled and sliced

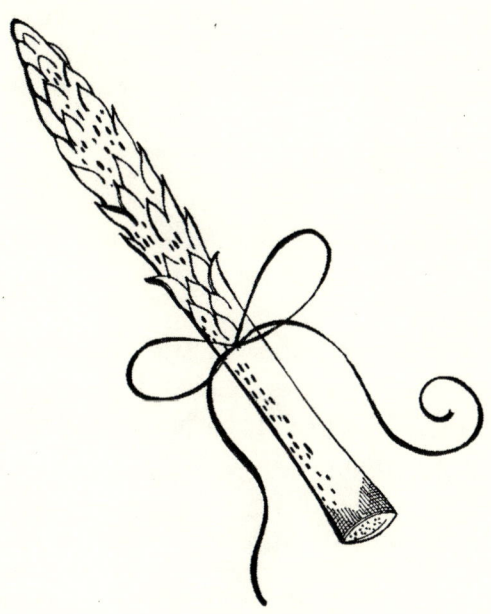

Lentils (and most legumes) freeze beautifully. Simply pour the remaining can (including liquid) into a freezer container and freeze. To use, either remove from the freezer first thing in the morning, or if you forget (which I usually do), defrost for 5-6 minutes in the microwave.

Lentil Loaf

My Mother-in-Law makes this from scratch: she starts with dried lentils. Her loaves always taste better than mine; I think the dried lentils give the loaf a better texture.

10 minute preparation
45 minute baking at 350°
Let sit 15 minutes before slicing
6 servings

Put all ingredients in food processor. Add a little liquid from the lentil can and process until the mixture is blended. The mixture should be moist (not wet). Pour into non-stick loaf tin that has been sprayed with vegetable spray. Bake 350° for 45 minutes.

If you're not going to use the whole loaf right away, leftovers can be frozen for later use. This loaf is delicious served cold and sliced as a sandwich filling.

2 cups canned lentils*, save liquid**
2 slices fresh bread, cubed
½ teas each: dried thyme, ground cumin, garlic powder
¼ teas black pepper
1 egg, beaten
1 small onion, chopped finely
½ lb medium or old cheddar, grated
1 teas Worcestershire sauce
Dash Tabasco
Salt to taste
1 tab soft butter

* place 1 cup dried lentils in a large sauce pan in 2 cups of water. Bring to a boil. Reduce heat to simmer and simmer 30-45 minutes until lentils are tender. Drain and rinse before using.

** If mixture is too dry, you can add canned tomato juice if you don't have enough liquid from the canned lentils (1/4 cup)

If you are bothered by gas after eating legumes, do not use the water used for cooking dried legumes or the liquid from the can. Use water instead. Thoroughly rinse cooked legumes and canned legumes before using to further reduce the incidence of gas.

Rice and Beans

This is a fast, one dish meal. When you make a pot of rice, make enough so you can have this dish later in the week—delicious!

Serve with fresh salsa on the side

5 minutes preparation
20 minutes cooking

Heat the oil in a large sauté pan. Add the onion and cook over medium low heat until the onion starts to soften (approx 5 minutes). Add the garlic and stir to combine. Sauté a few minutes more then add all the seasonings. Stir to combine.

Add the rice and beans**. Combine thoroughly and cook until the beans and rice are heated, approx 15 minutes (at this point, I usually put a lid on the sauté pan and turn the heat down to low, while I prepare the salsa).

Put one serving of rice and beans on each plate. Garnish with cilantro and green onion and put a serving of fresh salsa on the side.

** Add as many beans as you like: the ratio of bean to rice is up to you. I prefer the dish to be sprinkled with beans, but you may like higher bean content, in which case use ¾ to a full can of beans.

2 tab vegetable oil
¼ Spanish or sweet onion, diced

1 stalk celery, diced*
1 large clove garlic, minced
2 cups cooked white rice
½ 19 oz can black beans, drained and rinsed
1 teaspoon ground cumin
1 teaspoon ground ginger
½ teaspoon ground coriander
2 tab Worcestershire sauce
salt & pepper to taste

Garnish:
2 tab fresh chopped coriander
1-2 sliced green onion

*Peel the celery stalk with a vegetable peeler to remove the strings so they don't get caught in your teeth!

Fresh Salsa:
2 medium ripe tomatoes, chopped
2 green onions, thinly sliced
½ medium clove garlic, finely minced
½ green hot "finger" pepper or 1 jalapeño pepper (seeds removed), finely diced (wear rubber gloves when preparing hot peppers)
2 tab minced fresh coriander leaves
Juice from ¼ to ½ lemon or ½ lime
Salt to taste, dash of vegetable oil (optional)

In a medium bowl combine tomatoes, onions, garlic, hot pepper, and coriander. Sprinkle with lemon or lime juice (start with the lesser quantity and increase to suit your taste). Add a dash of vegetable oil (optional) and season with salt to taste. Stir to combine. Salsa is always tastier if you allow it to sit at room temperature for up to ½ hour.

Spicy Chick Peas

This recipe has a more complex flavor than Curried Chick Peas. It is suitable as part of an authentic Indian meal. If you're worried this dish might be too spicy, do not use the cayenne pepper or whole green chili, the dish will still be flavorful.

10 min preparation
20 min cooking
4 servings

Sauté the onions and garlic in the vegetable oil until the onions are transparent (about 5 minutes). Add the coriander, cumin, turmeric and cayenne. Stir in and sauté for a few minutes. Add the tomatoes, chick peas and 1 cup water to make a sauce. Add the toasted cumin, paprika, garam masala and lemon juice. Taste and add salt if necessary.

Cover and simmer (stirring occasionally) for approx 10 minutes. Add the chili and ginger, sauté for a few more minutes. Sprinkle with chopped coriander just before serving.

¼ cup vegetable oil
1 large sweet onion, diced
4 large cloves garlic, pressed
1 tab coriander seeds, ground
2 teas cumin seeds, ground
1 teas turmeric, ground
½ teas cayenne pepper
2 fresh tomatoes, cored and finely chopped
2 19 oz cans chick peas, drained

2 teas cumin seeds—toasted*, ground
1 teas paprika
1 teas garam masala**
Juice from ½ lemon
1 whole green chili, finely diced (wear gloves)
2 teas finely grated fresh ginger

Garnish:
2 tab fresh coriander, chopped

*to toast cumin seeds, place them in a small, dry, non-stick pan and heat over high heat until they begin to smoke (this only takes a few minutes). Stir and remove from heat immediately. Do not allow them to burn. They are toasted when you begin to see smoke and you can smell the cumin.

** Garam Masala is an Indian spice mixture found in Indian grocery stores or the specialty section of your local supermarket.

Spinach and Lentils

Spinach is one of the quickest vegetables to cook. In this dish, the washed, wet spinach is added directly to the pan. The pan is then covered and the spinach quickly steams.

If you want a stronger flavor, you can substitute Swiss chard. Use your kitchen scissors to remove the thick stems and to cut the spinach (or Swiss chard), into small, bite-sized pieces.

15 minutes preparation
15 minutes cooking
4 servings

Melt butter and vegetable oil in a large non-stick sauté pan over medium heat. Add the diced onion. Stir in the garlic and sauté for a few minutes until the onions start to soften.

Put the washed *wet* spinach on top of the onion/garlic mixture. Spread the spinach evenly over the pan. Sprinkle with a little sea salt (1/4 teas). Cover and simmer for a few minutes. Raise the lid and see if the spinach is starting to wilt. This should take approx. 5 minutes. Once the spinach has reduced in volume, add the tomatoes and Indian sauce. Stir all the ingredients together. If the sauce seems a little thick, add some V8 juice until the sauce is the consistency you like (you can always add a little more juice later if the sauce starts to thicken again).

Add the drained lentils and tofu. Gently stir all the ingredients together. Cover and reduce the heat to simmer and cook for approx. 5 minutes. Check the sauce consistency and add a little more V8 juice if necessary. Check the taste and season with a little more salt if necessary.

VEGETARIAN FOR A DAY

1 tab vegetable oil
1 tab butter
½ sweet onion, diced
2 large cloves garlic, finely diced
1 large bunch fresh spinach or Swiss chard—washed, large stems removed, chopped into bite-sized pieces
Sea salt to taste
2 tomatoes, diced
½ 400ml/13.5 oz bottle Indian Sauce such as Biryani
1 small 156 ml/5 oz can V8 juice or tomato juice
1 19 oz. can lentils, drained
¼ lb tofu—drained, dried with paper towel and cubed into 1/2 "cubes*

* You can substitute Paneer (Indian cheese) for tofu. You can omit tofu or paneer if you want to serve this as a side dish.

Legumes and Grains: Grain Recipes

Italian Polenta

This dish is very easy to make and delicious. You can substitute canned tomatoes for fresh. You can also try it with sweet red or green peppers instead of hot peppers. Fresh peppers may need a few additional minutes of cooking time.

10 minutes preparation
10 minutes cooking
4 servings

Bring vegetable stock to a boil in a medium non-stick saucepan. Gradually add the corn meal while stirring constantly with a wooden spoon. Reduce the heat to medium, add the chopped green onion and keep stirring for 2 minutes more until the liquid is completely absorbed. The mixture should look like thick pudding.

Transfer the mixture to a shallow bowl large enough to fit the polenta. Cover the bowl with a plate and let sit for 5 minutes. The polenta will become firm. Turn the mixture over onto the plate and cut the mound of polenta into four equal sections.

Heat the oil and butter in a large non-stick sauté pan. Fry the polenta pieces on medium heat until lightly browned on each side (every 30 seconds or so, turn the pieces using tongs). This should take a couple of minutes. Push the pieces to one side of the pan and add the onion, peppers, tomatoes, and garlic. Sauté for a few minutes until the tomatoes start to break down.

When the tomato mixture is cooked, sprinkle the crumbled feta on top of the tomato mixture. Stir to melt a little. Remove the pieces of polenta and place on a piece of paper towel to absorb some of the oil, and then transfer each piece to a plate.

Divide the tomato mixture into four equal portions and place a portion on each piece of polenta. Garnish with fresh basil and lemon juice (if using).

Season with salt and pepper and serve immediately.

2 ½ cups vegetable stock
1 cup corn meal
1 finely chopped green onion

2 tab olive oil
2 tab butter
½ sweet or red onion, thinly sliced
1 tab pickled jalapeño slices or hot banana pepper rings
2 diced fresh tomatoes
2 finely chopped large cloves garlic
3 fresh basil leaves, julienne
¼ cup Feta cheese, crumbed

Fresh lemon juice (optional)
Salt and pepper to taste

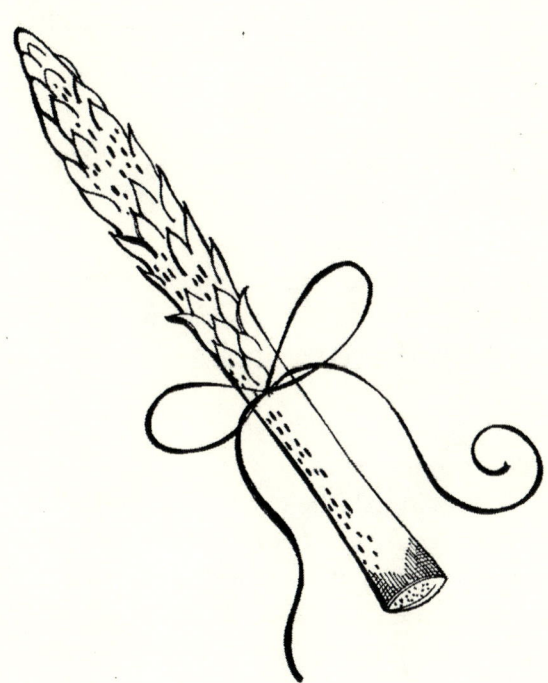

Cornmeal is made from corn that has been dried and ground. Corn is actually a grain, and not a vegetable!

Mexican Spoon Bread

This is delicious on its own but you can also make it when you have company over. Served with a bowl of vegetarian chili, it makes a great, casual meal.

10 minutes preparation
45 minutes baking at 400^0
8 servings

In a medium bowl, mix together corn, milk, butter and eggs. In a separate bowl, whisk together cornmeal, baking soda, baking powder and salt. Combine the two bowls together in a large bowl and mix thoroughly to make a batter.

Spray a 9" x 9" non-stick baking pan with vegetable spray (including the sides), and pour in half the batter. Tap the pan on the counter so the batter spreads out evenly and covers the bottom of the pan. Sprinkle with the pepper(s) and onions and half the cheese. Top with the rest of the batter, making sure the batter spreads over the surface, then sprinkle the surface with the rest of the cheese.

Bake. If possible, let cool 10 minutes, to make it easier to cut.

1 can cream style corn
¾ cup milk
¼ cup melted butter
2 eggs, beaten

1 cup cornmeal
½ teas baking soda
1 teas baking powder
1 teas salt

2 tab chopped pickled jalapeños or hot banana pepper rings, chopped
2 tab finely chopped sweet red pepper
2 tab finely chopped green onion

1 ½ cup grated medium cheddar

Quinoa

This is a great grain and can be used in place of rice or couscous in a lot of your favorite dishes.

2 min. rinsing
1 min. in the pressure cooker
10 min. resting
4 servings

Rinse the quinoa in *several* changes of water otherwise it will taste bitter. The fastest way to prepare it is in the pressure cooker. Bring the vegetable stock to a boil in the bottom of the cooker. Add the quinoa and snap the lid in place. Bring to high heat and cook under pressure for one minute. Let the pressure release gradually over 10 minutes.

1 ½ cups quinoa, washed and drained
2 ¼ cups vegetable stock

Stuffed Peppers

Use an assortment of sweet peppers (red, yellow, green & orange) and make a whole tray of these for a pretty presentation.

15 minutes preparation (Quinoa or Rice)
8 minutes cooking
45 minutes baking
One stuffed pepper is sufficient per person

Cut the tops (stem end) off the peppers—use a sharp paring knife to cut all the way around the tops at the widest part so that you have a nice big opening to fill * Remove seeds and white pith from inside the peppers. Set aside until ready to fill.

In a large non-stick sauté pan, melt butter over medium heat. Add diced vegetables, garlic and spices. Sauté over medium heat approx. 8 minutes until vegetables are tender. Add the diced tomatoes and prepared quinoa or rice.

Stuff the prepared peppers—don't pack the filling, just fill loosely. Stand the stuffed peppers in an ovenproof dish (I use a small lasagna pan that has been sprayed with cooking spray).

Bake in a pre-heated 350^0 oven for 45 minutes. Carefully remove from the pan using sturdy tongs, and place one on each plate.

Variation—use corn instead of zucchini (1 cup) and substitute ½ tab chili powder with ¼ teas cinnamon for the curry powder and cumin for a Mexican flavor.

Variation—cut the pepper in half *horizontally* and fill. Cover with foil and bake. Check for doneness after 30 minutes of baking.

Variation—when peppers have finished baking, remove the pan from the oven and top each pepper with approx. 1 tab grated cheddar. Return to the oven and broil until the cheese melts (this will only take a few minutes, so keep an eye on it so the cheese doesn't burn.)

Cooked Quinoa (see basic recipe) Prepare quinoa as basic recipe directs.

Assorted colored peppers
2 tab butter
½ sweet onion, finely chopped
1 stalk celery, peeled and finely chopped
1 large carrot, peeled and finely chopped
1 small zucchini, peeled and finely chopped
1 large clove garlic, pressed
1 tab curry powder
1 teas ground roasted cumin
½ can diced tomatoes

Vegetable Biryani

There are endless variations of this dish. Basically its rice with vegetables. After you've made it a few times, substitute your own choices of vegetables. You can even make it with leftover cooked vegetables if you want to use them up.

If you're in a hurry, partly cook the vegetables in the microwave (in a small container, with a little water). This will reduce the overall cooking time but the flavor won't be as good.

10 minutes preparation
10 minutes frying
15 minutes cooking (Rice)

Rinse rice in a colander under cold running water until water runs clear.

Heat the oil in a large non-stick sauté pan over medium heat. When the oil is hot, add onions and sauté a few minutes. When the onions are soft, add all the seasonings and cook for a minute or two until you begin to smell the spice aroma.

Reduce heat slightly and add the vegetables. Stir for a few minutes. When the vegetables are starting to cook (after about 5-7 minutes), add the water. Bring to a boil then add rice. Stir to combine with the vegetables. Reduce heat to simmer and cover pan. Cook over low heat for about 15 minutes (do not remove the lid until 15 minutes is up—if it sounds like its boiling instead of simmering, reduce the heat a little more). After 15 minutes, check that the rice is tender and the vegetables are all cooked. If the rice is not cooked to your liking, cover and cook a few minutes more. If the rice looks like its getting too dry, add a couple of tablespoons of water before returning to the heat.

½ sweet onion, diced
½ small cauliflower, cut in bite-sized pieces
2 potatoes, peeled cut in small cubes
1 lb green beans, tips removed, cut in 1" pieces
1 cup frozen peas
1 large carrot, peeled cut in small pieces

Seasonings:
1 cup white rice
2 cups water
2 tab vegetable oil
¼ teas turmeric, chili powder, cumin
1 teas salt
½ teas garam masala (optional)
2 bay leaves
2 cardamom pods, remove seeds and use them (or ¼ teas cardamom powder)

1 cinnamon stick (or ¼ teas cinnamon powder)
1" piece fresh ginger, peeled and grated
¼ cup golden raisins
¼ cup cashews

Introduction to Meat Alternatives

Most meat alternatives are made from soy. The final product is designed to look and act like a meat product. There are many different vegetarian meat look a likes: including hotdogs, burgers, sausages, bacon, deli slices, "chiken nuggets," "chiken burgers."

My favorite product is veggie ground round. It looks and acts like hamburger. It can be used anywhere you would use hamburger. The taste and texture will fool even the most avid meat eater. The advantage to this product (and other meat alternatives) is that they are usually pre-cooked so they are easy to prepare. Most required light grilling or re-heating only. You do not have to drain off any fat as you would with real hamburger.

When using veggie ground round, remember to add it during the last few minutes of cooking. It is not necessary or recommended to overcook these products.

Depending on the dish you would like to make, you can substitute veggie burgers. Most contain vegetables and beans. Read the labels first before buying to decide if you're likely to enjoy the taste. Try one prepared using the recommended method on the package, then decide if they can be used in some of your dishes.

Two other meat alternatives worth mentioning are **Tempeh** and **Seitan.**

Tempeh originated in Indonesia and is made from whole soybeans. It has a higher content of protein, dietary fiber and vitamins than tofu.

Seitan is made from wheat gluten. It is quite high in protein and low in fat.

These products can be substituted in recipes using hamburger, stir frying, stews, soups and sandwiches.

Meat Alternatives: Recipes

Burritos

This is one of my favorite meals. I usually make fresh salsa to go with it. I often serve it with a side of leftover rice and a simple green salad.

This recipe makes enough to fill two large size tortillas or four small size tortillas. Depending on the number of tortillas you are using, divide the burrito mixture accordingly.

15 minute preparation
2 minute microwave
Serves 2-4 servings

Salsa:

Prepare the salsa first to allow the flavors to develop. Mix all the ingredients together in a medium ceramic bowl. Set aside at room temperature.

Burritos:

Place 2 tab vegetable oil in a large, non-stick skillet. Add the diced vegetables and sauté until soft (5-8 min). Add veggie ground round or burgers (if adding burgers, break them up with a wooden spoon). Add chili powder and Tabasco sauce combine with vegetables. Sauté another 2 minutes. Sprinkle with fresh coriander and set aside. Prepare the sauce.

Sauce:

Combine all the ingredients in a bowl. Taste and adjust seasoning if necessary.

To Assemble:

Place a tortilla on a microwaveable plate. Take one serving of the burrito mixture and spoon it onto one side of a tortilla (do not overfill or you won't be able to roll it up). Roll the tortilla, so that the seam is on the bottom of the plate. Spoon a portion of sauce over the burrito to cover it along the top. Sprinkle with a portion of the cheese. Loosely wrap the plate with plastic wrap. Microwave on high 2 min or until the cheese melts. Serve each prepared burrito with a little salsa on the side.

* Look for burgers containing pinto beans for an authentic Mexican flavor (substitute black bean burgers).

** Look for Chipotle Tabasco© sauce for an authentic Mexican flavor

Salsa:
1 or two ripe tomatoes, core removed and diced
2 spring onions or 2 tab finely diced mild sweet onion
½ lime, juiced
½ pickled jalapeño, finely diced or to taste (substitute 1 fresh green chili, seeds removed and finely diced)
Fresh coriander—finely chopped (about 2 tab) or more to taste
Salt to taste

Burritos:
Oil for frying
½ cup mushrooms, finely chopped
¼ red or green sweet pepper, finely chopped
1-2 tab chili powder
1 celery stalk, finely chopped (optional)
½ mild sweet onion, finely chopped
½ med zucchini, finely chopped
Handful coriander leaves—finely chopped (approx ¼ cup)
Dash of Tabasco sauce
½ package veggie ground round or 2 Mexican style * veggie burgers, chopped

1 cup grated cheddar (mild or medium)
1 package flour tortillas (large or small size)

Sauce:
½ 19 oz can tomato sauce
1 tab hickory BBQ sauce
Dash of Worcestershire and Tabasco**
½ tab chili powder

Italian Meatballs

For a nice change, serve these meatballs with egg noodles instead of spaghetti. Pair this dish with an Italian salad.

Baking the meatballs instead of frying them reduces the amount of oil used.

15 min preparation
20 min baking at 350°
4 servings

Put all meatball ingredients in the food processor and start to process. Add a little of the stock (1 or 2 tab) if the mixture appears too dry. Process until the ingredients are blended.

Spoon out 2 tab of the mixture and roll into a ball. You should have enough to make 12 to 16 "bite-sized" balls (each no more than 1" diameter).

Spray a non-stick cookie sheet with vegetable spray and put the balls on the sheet, spaced evenly apart. Bake in the centre of the oven for 20 minutes.

Cook the egg noodles as the package directs. Drain and set aside.

While the meatballs are baking, prepare the sauce: Drizzle a large non-stick sauté pan with oil (1 or 2 tab). Sauté the mushrooms over medium heat for a couple of minutes. Add the garlic and sauté 1 minute more. Add the tomatoes, oregano and stock. Bring to a boil. Add the cornstarch mixture and stir until the sauce thickens. Reduce the heat to low.

Add the baked meatballs. Cover and simmer about five minutes until combined. When ready to serve, sprinkle with fresh basil.

Divide the noodles evenly between four plates. Top the noodles with the meatballs and serve immediately.

Meatballs:
1 package Italian style veggie ground round
1 egg white
¼ cup wheat gluten
2 tab Italian bread crumbs
¼ cup freshly grated parmesan
1 large clove garlic, minced
1 tab Worcestershire
1 teas dried oregano
½ teas dried red pepper flakes
2 tab vegetarian beef-flavored stock*

Sauce:
Vegetable oil for the pan
½ pound mushrooms, sliced
1 large clove garlic, minced
2 cups canned plum tomatoes, chopped and drained
1 teas dried oregano (or Italian seasoning)
2 cups (less 3 tab) vegetarian beef-flavored stock
1 ½ tab cornstarch (dissolved in 1 tab vegetarian beef-flavored stock)

Garnish with fresh basil leaves that have been finely sliced

4 servings dried egg noodles—cooked as package directs.

*if you can't find this, use prepared onion soup as the stock.

Laureen's Chili

I often serve this Chili to meat eaters. They really enjoy it and don't realize they are not eating ground beef. It's very flavorful. You can vary the degree of heat by altering the amount of chili powder.

I highly recommend using my recipe for chili powder—the taste is superior to store-bought.

15 minute preparation
10 + minutes cooking
4 servings

Cut the tomatoes into large pieces, I usually use my kitchen scissors and cut the tomatoes while still in the can. Save the liquid from the cans. Dice all the vegetables close to the same size if possible (this will help them cook more evenly).

Put olive oil in the bottom of a large Dutch oven. Sauté the garlic and onions 3-4 minutes to soften. Add the diced vegetables and sauté about 5 minutes until vegetables are cooked.

Add the veggie ground round and seasonings. Sauté another 2-3 minutes to incorporate. Add tomatoes and their liquid and tomato juice. Add the canned beans and lemon juice, if using. Stir thoroughly. Add salt (if necessary), to taste.

Cover and simmer at least 10 minutes (20 minutes is ideal).

Serve over steamed rice or egg noodles. Top each serving with grated cheddar and/or fresh coriander.

VEGETARIAN FOR A DAY

This chili freezes beautifully.

2-3 tab olive oil
2 cloves garlic (pressed)
½ sweet onion, diced
½ cup zucchini, diced
½ cup mushrooms, diced
1 stalk celery, diced
½ cup cooked green beans
1 medium carrot, diced
¼ sweet red or green pepper, diced

½ package veggie ground round***
1 teas ground cumin
2-3 tab chili powder
1 28 oz can whole tomatoes
1 14 oz can whole tomatoes
½ can pinto beans*
½ can kidney beans
1 tab fresh lemon juice (optional)
½ 14 oz can tomato juice**
Salt to taste

Optional Garnish:

Grated cheddar
Finely chopped fresh coriander

Chili Powder:
¼ teas red pepper flakes
1 ½ teas whole cumin
1 teas whole coriander
1 teas cocoa powder
2 teas dried oregano
1 teas cinnamon

Grind all ingredients in a spice or coffee grinder. For more heat, add 1/8 teas cayenne pepper.

*   Try other types of beans for variety such as black or brown beans, increase the quantity if you like

**   Vary the amount of juice depending on the consistency you like your chili to be (thick or thin)

***Use textured vegetable protein Mexican burgers as a substitute (prepare as package directs), then crumble.

"Meat" Sauce

Use this sauce for pasta or Sloppy Joes. This sauce has a meaty consistency because I use "Hamburger" alternative. These packages of "hamburger" are sold in the vegetarian deli section of most supermarkets. You can use this "hamburger" in any dish you would normally use real meat hamburger.

15 minutes preparation
20 minutes cooking
4 servings

Pour olive oil into the bottom of a large, heavy saucepan. Set the heat to medium-low. Add chopped onion and garlic. Stir until lightly browned (about 2 minutes). Add zucchini, sweet red pepper, hot banana peppers and mushrooms. Sauté 5 minutes until the vegetables are starting to cook. Add the can of tomatoes (reserve some of the liquid) Chop them with a knife (or kitchen shears) when they are in the pan. Add tomato paste, wine, Worcestershire sauce, bay leaves, red pepper flakes, cumin, oregano and "hamburger." Stir to combine. Cover the pan and cook, Stirring occasionally. If the sauce becomes too thick for your liking, add some (or all) of the reserved liquid from the can of tomatoes. Simmer approx. 20 minutes until the vegetables are cooked. Season to taste with salt & pepper. Just before serving, sprinkle with freshly chopped basil.

¼ cup olive or vegetable oil
½ large Spanish onion, chopped
3 or 4 cloves garlic, minced
½ medium size zucchini, peeled & diced
1/3 sweet red pepper, diced

1 tab hot banana pepper rings, chopped
1 cup chopped mushrooms
1 28 oz can whole Italian tomatoes
1 small can tomato paste
½ cup dry red wine (optional)
dash of Worcestershire sauce
2 bay leaves
pinch red pepper flakes
pinch cumin powder
1 tab dry oregano flakes
½ package "ground beef" alternative
salt & pepper

Garnish:
1/3 cup chopped fresh basil

¼ cup olive or vegetable oil
28 oz. can whole Italian tomatoes
dash of Worcestershire sauce
½ cup dry red wine (optional)
½ medium size zucchini, diced
1 tab hot banana pepper rings, chopped
¼ cup chopped fresh basil
2 bay leaves
pinch red pepper flakes
1 small can tomato paste
½ large Spanish onion, chopped
1 cup chopped mushrooms
¼ sweet red pepper, diced
pinch cumin powder
1 tab dry oregano
½ package "ground beef" alternative

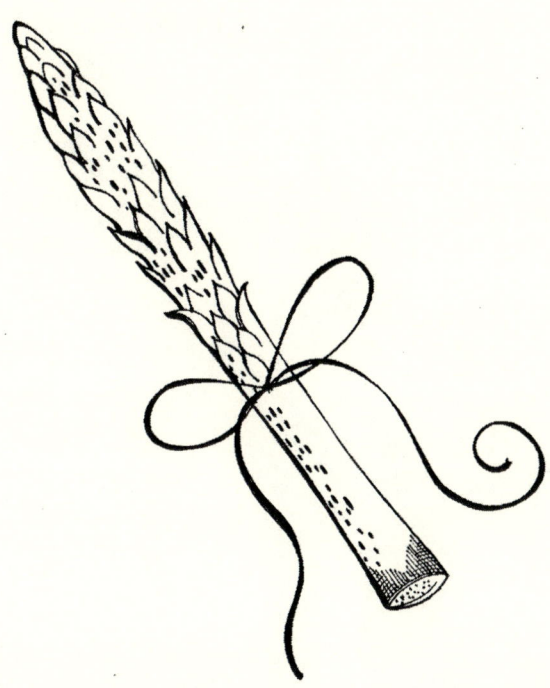

Quick Tip: tomato paste can be frozen so you can use it as you need it. Simply remove both ends of the can, cover the ends with a piece of plastic wrap and place the can in the freezer. When ready to use, thaw for a couple of minutes and push out the required amount of tomato paste, cut it off with a sharp knife, re-cover the ends of the can and return it to the freezer.

Pineapple Meatballs

These are good with plain white rice or fried rice. I like to serve them with lightly steamed snow peas.

For a fancy presentation, buy a whole pineapple. Cut in half lengthwise. Cut out all the pineapple from one half, leaving a curved boat shape. (Use the fresh pineapple for the recipe). Fill the pineapple half with the cooked mixture and place on a platter, surrounded by rice.

15 min preparation
20 min baking at 350º
4 servings

Pre-heat the oven to 350º

Put all the meatball ingredients in a food processor and process until blended.

Spoon out 2 tab of the mixture and roll into a ball about 1" diameter. This recipe should make 12 to 16 balls*.

Spray a non-stick cookie sheet with vegetable spray and put the balls on the sheet, spacing them evenly apart. Bake in the centre of the oven for 20 minutes.

While the meatballs are baking, prepare the sauce: In a large non-stick sauté pan, over medium heat, sauté sweet red pepper, zucchini, onion and garlic in oil until softened (3-5 minutes). Add the diced tomato.

Put all the other sauce ingredients (except the pineapple) into a blender and blend until smooth.

Pour the blender contents over the sautéed vegetables in the pan. Stir over medium heat until the sauce begins to thicken, about 3 minutes. Add the pineapple chunks (and red pepper flakes if using) and the baked meatballs. Cover and simmer about five minutes more and serve.

* I like the meatballs to be "bite-sized" (No more than 1" diameter).

Meatballs:
1 package Italian style veggie ground round
1 egg white
¼ cup wheat gluten
2 tab bread crumbs
2 teas mustard
2 teas Worcestershire
¼ teas each onion flakes, garlic powder, ground ginger
1 tab toasted sesame seeds
1 tab soy sauce
1 teas chili garlic sauce

Sauce:
2 tab vegetable oil
½ cup sweet red pepper, chopped
½ cup zucchini
1 med sweet onion, diced
3 cloves garlic
1 diced tomato

1 cup pineapple juice*
1 ½ tab cornstarch (dissolve in 2 tab of the pineapple juice)
½ cup brown sugar

¼ cup white wine vinegar
3 tab soy sauce
2 tab tomato paste
1 teas sesame oil

1 cup pineapple chunks
Sprinkling red pepper flakes (optional)

*If you buy canned pineapple chunks or pieces, the can may contain enough juice to make 1 cup.

Stroganoff

This is a creamy, delicious meat-free version of the classic. I like it with egg noodles, rice or mashed potatoes—your choice.

20 minutes preparation
Serves 4

In a large non-stick sauté pan, sauté the mushrooms and onions in oil until the onions are translucent. Add the garlic, and stir a few times for about a minute. Crumble the veggie ground round into the pan so that it resembles hamburger. Add Worcestershire and soy sauce. Season the mixture with spices. Stir for one minute until blended. Stir in the can of mushroom soup.

Once the soup has been incorporated, taste it and decide if you want the mixture thinner or richer tasting.

If you want it thinner add the red wine or stock. Simmer 5 extra minutes.

If you want it richer, add the sour cream or yoghurt instead of the wine or stock.

Finish the dish with a dash of paprika, and one chopped green onion sprinkled on top.

Tip: for an east Indian flavor, add 1 ½ tab curry powder (mild or medium), and garnish with unsweetened shredded coconut (1-2 tablespoons)

¼ cup vegetable oil
½ lb fresh mushrooms, chopped
½ sweet onion, diced
1-2 cloves garlic, finely chopped
1 package veggie ground round or 3 veggie patties, broken up
Dash Worcestershire
Dash soy sauce
1-2 teas. Italian seasoning or oregano
1 can condensed Cream of Mushroom soup

Optional:
¼ cup red wine or
¼ vegetable stock or
¼ cup sour cream or yoghurt

Garnish (optional):
Dash sweet paprika
1 green onion, finely chopped

Sweet & Sour Cabbage Rolls

Very traditional cabbage rolls, but instead of ground beef, we substitute veggie ground round. No one will notice the difference!

This is a good recipe to make on the weekend as it takes a while to cook.

20 min preparation
½ hour cooking (cabbage only)
1 1/2 hours cooking
6 servings

Remove the centre "rib" from each leaf of cabbage. You can cut it out or use scissors. This will make rolling easier later. Put the leaves in a large pot of boiling water and boil until tender, approx. ½ hour. Drain the pot and cool the leaves until they are cool enough to handle them (to speed up the cooling process put the boiled leaves in a colander and run cold water over them. Dry each leaf with a paper towel).

Mix the filling ingredients together in a large bowl. Put approx. 2 tab of filling in the centre of each leaf. Lift the edge of the leaf and fold it over the filling. Then fold both ends of the leaf in towards the centre of the roll. This will prevent the filling falling out the ends. Continue rolling until the leaf is rolled up and the filling is covered. Put a toothpick in the centre of each completed roll to hold it closed.

Place the "Bottom" ingredients in the bottom of the Dutch oven.

Place the cabbage rolls on top of the "bottom" ingredients.

Mix the sauce ingredients in a large bowl and pour it over the rolls to cover them. Put a lid on the Dutch oven and cook over low heat for 1 ½ hours.

1 medium green cabbage

Filling:
½ package veggie ground round or two mildly flavored veggie burgers, broken into small pieces (to resemble hamburger)*
¼ cup cooked & cooled rice**
1 large sweet onion, finely chopped
1 tab fresh lemon juice
1 teas salt & pepper, paprika

Bottom of Dutch oven:
Oil to coat bottom
Thinly sliced onion (about 1/2 small cooking onion)
Salt & pepper
Dash of paprika
½ cup water

Sauce:
¼ cup fresh lemon juice (approx. 4 lemons)
2 10 oz. Cans Cream of Tomato Soup (condensed)
1 cup brown sugar

* For a different flavor, you can substitute ½ can of lentils for the veggie ground round.
** You can use leftover cooked rice

Introduction to Vegetables

Fresh vegetables are an important part of a healthy diet. It is recommended we eat 3-5 servings of vegetables a day. If you have a salad and/or a bowl of vegetable soup for lunch followed by one or two vegetables on your plate at dinner, you're doing well.

To boost your daily vegetable intake, throw some carrot and celery sticks in your lunch box to snack on or drink a vegetable juice at lunch or dinner. Add greens (such as lettuce or baby spinach) or sprouts to your sandwiches.

I always buy vegetables "in season." This is easy at the end of the summer when local harvests are plentiful. It can be more of a challenge in winter as vegetables and fruit can come from half way around the world. Try to shop at a green grocer where turnover is frequent and the vegetables are fresh.

Wash all vegetables thoroughly. Peel the skins off whenever possible. Raw vegetables contain the most nutrients.

Should you buy organic?

If you have access to organic, and you can afford it, the answer is yes. I personally find very little difference in taste but there are other factors to consider. The number one factor is the use of pesticides. At this point, we don't know the full consequences of eating food that has been grown with the use of pesticides[6]. Organically grown produce is grown without the use of residual toxic chemicals, using ecologically friendly substances to improve soil and the method of farming is considered to be "earth friendly." Organic also means no GMO's (Genetically Modified Organisms)[7]

Are raw vegetables better for you than cooked?

Yes and No. Vegetables containing vitamin C should not be cooked as heat destroys vitamin C. However, cooking breaks down the tough fibers of some vegetables, making the nutrients easier to digest and absorb.

If you have to cook vegetables, they should be boiled for a short period of time in a small amount of water to retain more of their nutrients and to make them easier to digest.

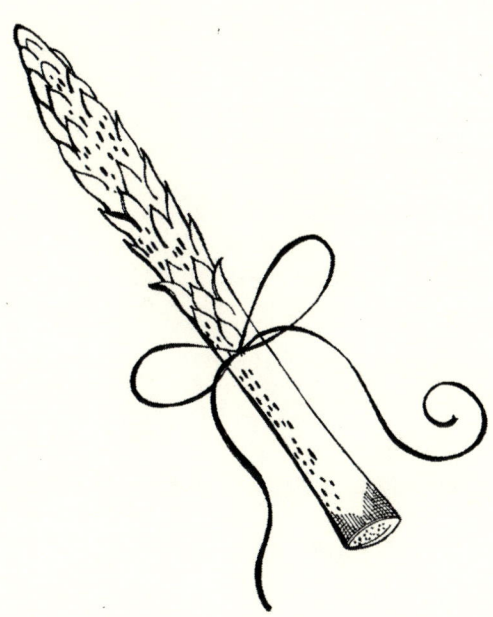

Food Fact: Carrots contain carotenoids which are antioxidants (antioxidants fight certain cancers). We absorb only 3-4% of carotenoids from raw carrots as compared to 15-20% from cooked carrots!

Vegetables: Recipes

Bok Choi Stir Fry

You can make this tasty, quick meal with pretty much any dark vegetable such as broccoli, green beans, asparagus, rapini or other varieties of Asian greens.

I like the "baby" bok choi which is small and tender. If you go to an Asian market, you may be lucky enough to find Bok Choi "Buds" which are even smaller (and sweeter!).

5 minutes preparation
10 minutes stir-frying

Whisk all the dressing ingredients together in a medium bowl or put all ingredients in a blender and blend at high speed for 30 seconds.

Put the oil in a wok or large non-stick sauté pan. Heat the wok on high until the oil smokes. Add the Bok Choi and stir-fry a minute. When it begins to wilt, add the bean sprouts. Stir-fry together for approximately 5 minutes.

Give the dressing a final whisk (or spin in the blender), then quickly add to the center of the wok (push all the ingredients up the side to make a "well"). When the liquid starts to boil add the cornstarch mixture if you would like a thick sauce over your vegetables. If you just want to season the vegetables with the dressing, omit the cornstarch mixture and just mix the dressing in until all the vegetables are coated and serve.

Dressing:
1 ½ tablespoon Tamari soy sauce
2 tablespoons sesame oil
juice from ¼ lemon (or more if desired)
¼ large clove garlic, finely grated
1" piece fresh peeled ginger, finely grated
pinch sugar
1 tablespoon toasted sesame seeds
sprinkle salt
sprinkle red chili flakes (optional)
1 tablespoon cornstarch mixed with 2 tablespoons water to form a white liquid (optional)
2 tablespoons vegetable oil
4 Bok Choi, rinsed and coarsely chopped*
1-2 cups fresh bean sprouts

*if you are using Baby Bok Choi or the younger, "Buds," you don't need to chop it if you don't want to.

Broccoli Bake

Served over egg noodles or mashed potatoes, Broccoli Bake makes a main course. This is also a very satisfying side dish.

10 min preparation
20 min baking 350°
6 servings

Boil the broccoli in a medium saucepan in a small amount of salted water. Boil the broccoli just until tender, about 5 minutes (do not overcook). Drain off all the water. Mix the broccoli with all the other ingredients (except the cracker crumbs).

Pour the mixture into an ovenproof casserole that has been sprayed with vegetable oil spray. Top it with cracker crumbs. Bake at 350° for 20 minutes.

1 large broccoli, cut into bite-size pieces
¼ cup finely diced onion
1 can condensed cream of mushroom soup
1 250 ml container sour cream
1 cup medium or old cheddar, grated

10 vegetable thin crackers finely crumbled (I put the crackers in a sealed baggie and roll over them with a rolling pin until they are crumbled).

Cauliflower Casserole

I often serve this pie as a main course. One slice is very satisfying and because it contains protein, vegetables and starch, you don't need to serve anything else. This casserole is time-consuming to make so save it for special occasions.

The addition of the eggs helps to bind the cauliflower to the "scalloped" potatoes.

30 minutes preparation
Pie: 30-40 minutes baking
4-6 Servings

Pre-heat your oven to 450°

Spray an oval casserole dish with vegetable spray. Set aside.

Sauté the chopped onion in the oil and butter over medium high heat in a large non-stick saucepan until the onion is transparent (about 3 minutes). Add the cauliflower, salt & pepper, thyme vinegar and basil and sauté approx. 2 minutes until the cauliflower starts to soften. Add the garlic and combine. Transfer this mixture to the casserole and spread it evenly over the bottom.

Pour the well beaten eggs over the cauliflower mixture.

To make the sauce:

Combine the butter and flour in a non-stick saucepan over medium heat. Stir with a wooden spoon until the butter melts into the flour and makes a thick paste. Slowly stir in the milk and cream (you may need to increase the heat slightly). When it starts to thicken (3-5 minutes), add the Parmesan. Stir until it melts. Season with salt & pepper and a little nutmeg. Remove the sauce from the heat so it doesn't get too thick to pour.

Cover the cauliflower/egg mixture with a thin layer of potatoes. Top with a thin layer of onions. Lightly salt and pepper the surface. Add another layer of potato and onion, salt and pepper again. Now add ½ the sauce—pour over the entire surface if you can. Repeat the potato/onion layers (including salt & pepper) until the potato/onion is finished. Top with the remaining ½ of the sauce.

Just before baking, sprinkle the surface with the grated cheddar. Place the casserole on a non-stick baking sheet (in case it bubbles over) and bake until firm (30-40 minutes—check after 30 minutes).

Let cool 10-15 minutes if possible before slicing.

3 tab chopped sweet onion
1 tab vegetable oil
1 tab butter
½ medium-sized cauliflower, cut into bite-sized pieces
¼ teas each salt, pepper
1 teas fresh thyme leaves chopped (approx 5 stalks)
1 teas white vinegar
Fresh basil leaves, chopped (approx 4 large leaves)
2 extra large eggs*, well beaten
¼ of a whole peeled sweet onion sliced into thin rounds (you may not need all of it)
1 large clove garlic—finely chopped

Sauce:
2 tab butter
2 tab flour
¾ cup 2% milk
¼ cup 5% cream
4 tablespoons grated fresh Parmesan
salt & pepper
sprinkle of fresh nutmeg (optional)

2 medium sized baking potatoes—peeled and very thinly sliced**
½ cup medium or old cheddar cheese, grated

*try to choose organic, free-range eggs (they taste better and are a more humane choice)
**A Mandolin would be the ideal tool for thin slices

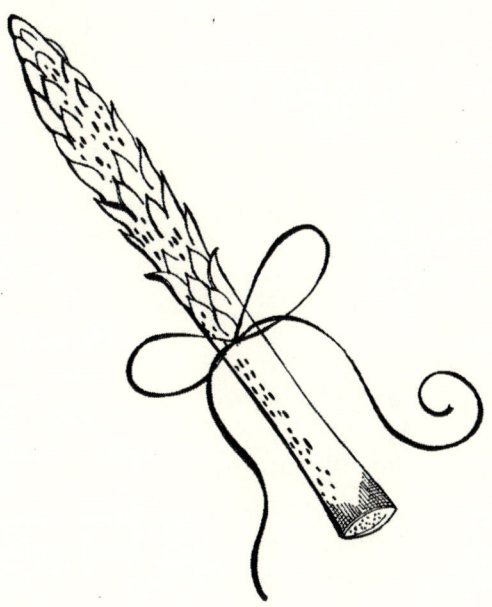

Cooking Tip: Remember to spray right up the sides of the dish including the handles. Even if the food splatters in the oven, it will still be easier to clean the dish if you spray it completely.

Eggplant Parmesana

If you don't like eggplant, try other varieties of eggplant such as Asian or Indian or look for small (baby) Italian eggplants. They will be more tender and the skin not so tough.

10 minutes preparation
30 minutes baking at 350°
10 minutes cooling
6 servings

Preheat the oven to 350°

Dip each eggplant slice in the beaten egg, then coat the eggplant slice with breadcrumbs. Fry the slices in a non-stick pan in oil heated over med-high heat. Fry the eggplant in batches so as not to overcrowd the pan (overcrowding will reduce the heat of the oil and will cause the slices to be soggy instead of crisp). Brown each slice on both sides (about 2-3 minutes frying per side). Drain each batch on paper towels. When you're finished with the oil, remove all but ½ tablespoon from the pan.

When all the eggplant is fried, place half the slices in the bottom of a 9" x 13" lasagna dish that has been sprayed with vegetable spray.

Sauté the garlic in the pan for one minute. Add the tomatoes and seasonings. Sauté approx. 5 minutes until the tomatoes start to fry.

Spoon half the tomato mixture over the eggplant. Sprinkle with half of both types of cheese. Add the remaining eggplant in a layer. Add the second half of the tomato mixture and top with the remaining cheeses.

Place the lasagna dish on a non-stick cookie sheet in the oven. Bake 30 minutes until the cheese starts to bubble and the surface is browned. Let cool 10 minutes before serving (this cooling will allow you to slice the eggplant easier as it will hold together better when cooled a little). Garnish each serving with a sprig of fresh basil.

1 egg, well beaten in a small bowl
6 small eggplants, tops and bottoms removed and sliced into ¼" thick slices
¾ cup Italian breadcrumbs, in a small bowl
1/3 cup (or less) olive oil

2 cloves garlic, pressed
1 28 oz can ground Italian tomatoes
½ teas dried oregano
Salt & pepper to taste
Pinch red pepper flakes (or to taste)

1 cup grated mozzarella or other mild cheese
¼ cup freshly grated parmesan

Garnish (Optional):
Fresh basil

Fried Eggplant

I never used to like eggplant until I started making this dish. The secret is the extra drying time given to the eggplant pieces. This allows all the excess moisture to be drawn from the eggplant, resulting in crispy (not greasy) eggplant.

This dish goes with Middle-Eastern, Italian and Indian dishes. You can also serve it in the summer with other cold salads, in particular lentil salad.

Overnight drying of eggplant (or at least 2 hours)
5 min preparation time for vegetables
15 min frying time
4 servings

Prepare the eggplant as directed. Put the slices in a colander and sprinkle with salt. Rest a heavy bowl on top of the eggplant (I usually fill a ceramic bowl with water) and leave the eggplant overnight if possible (or at least 2 hours). Rinse the pieces under cold running water to remove salt and pat them dry with paper towels. You're now ready to fry them.

Pour enough oil into a large non-stick skillet to cover the bottom to a depth of about ¼." Heat the oil on medium high. When its hot, slip each piece of dried eggplant into the oil using your long handled tongs. Cover the surface with pieces but don't overcrowd so each piece fries evenly. When the pieces are golden brown (in a minute or two), remove them with tongs and place on paper towel to drain. Do the next batch until all the pieces have been fried.

Pour off most of the oil, leaving approx. 1 teas in the bottom of the skillet. Quickly fry the onion rings and remove them when they are browned and softened. Drain them on paper towel.

Add the tomatoes and fry the slices until they start to break up. Add the vinegar and mix into the tomatoes. Remove from heat.

To serve, place all the eggplant pieces on your serving dish. Top with onion rings and tomatoes. Sprinkle the top with the minced garlic. Serve immediately or cool to room temperature if you're serving it with other salads.

2 lbs small eggplant (the smaller the better)—slice off the tops and bottoms, and peel off the skin in 1" intervals. Cut the eggplant into ¼" slices

sea salt

½ sweet onion, peeled and sliced into thin rings
2 ripe tomatoes, remove cores and slice ¼" thick
1 tab balsamic vinegar
1 clove garlic, finely minced
Oil for frying

Gourmet Pizza

Once you start making homemade pizza, you'll never want to order take-out again. Each person can have their own pizza with toppings of their choice. All you have to do is think "outside the box" (the pizza box, that is). Served with a salad, this is a healthy meal.

My favorite pizza crust is Indian Nan bread; it is just the right thickness.

10 minutes preparation
8 minutes baking at 450°

Choose one or more types of bread to use as a crust. Prepare your pizza tray by brushing with olive oil. Brush the bottom of the crust with olive oil.

Put a thin layer of tomato sauce over the crust. Spread evenly. Top with seasoning(s)

Evenly distribute the toppings. Don't overload!

Sprinkle on 2 or more types of cheese.

Bake in pre-heated oven until you see the toppings start to bubble.

If serving with a salad, one pizza should be enough for each person.

Remember: with gourmet pizza, less is more. Don't overload or you won't taste all the flavors and the crust may not support the weight (especially if you use tortillas or pita)

Lay vegetables on their flat side to make slicing easier

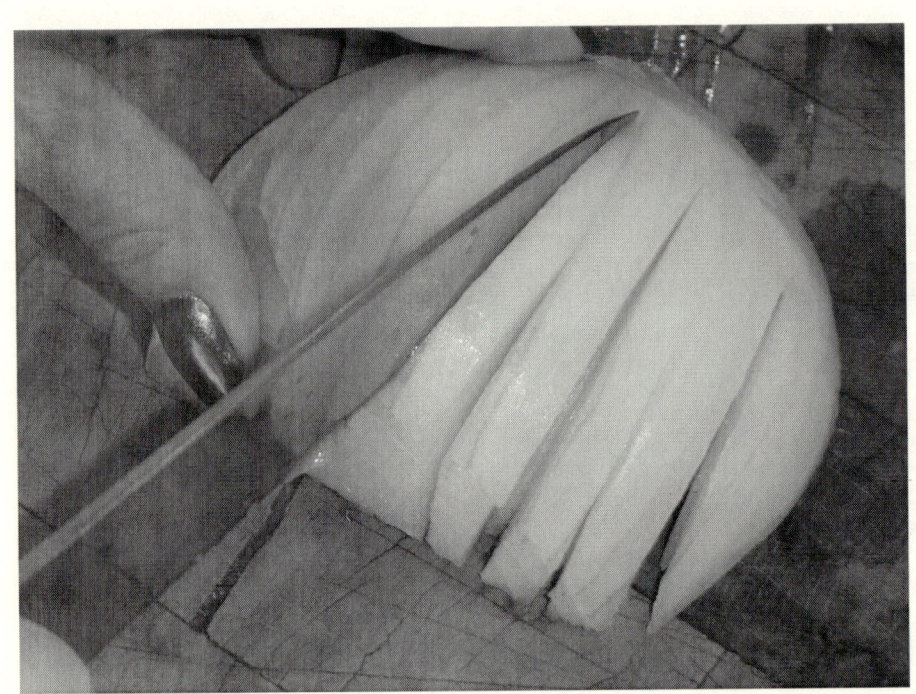

Make long parallel cuts in an onion

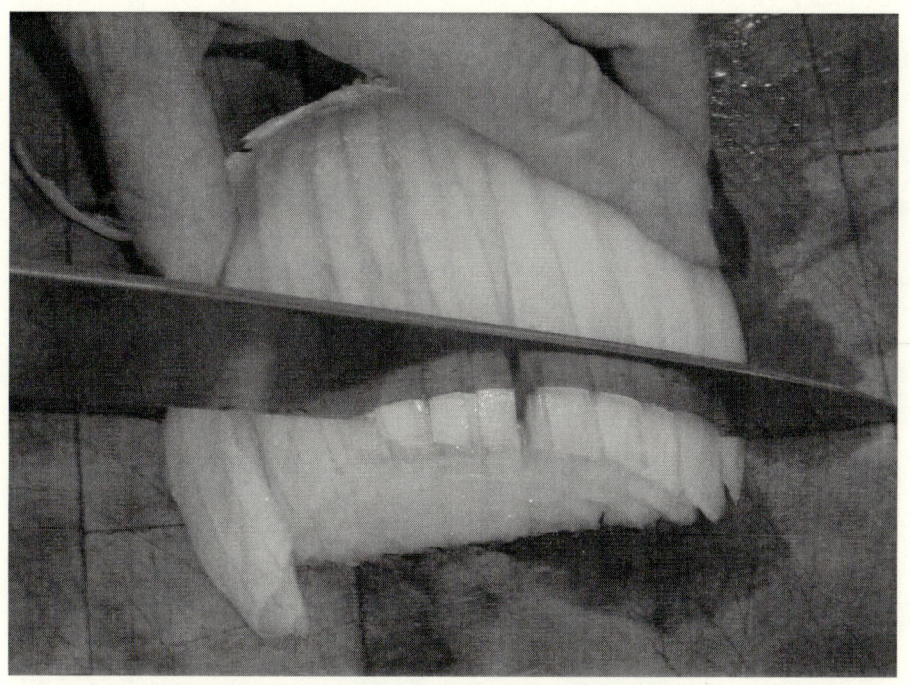
Then turn the onion sideways and dice

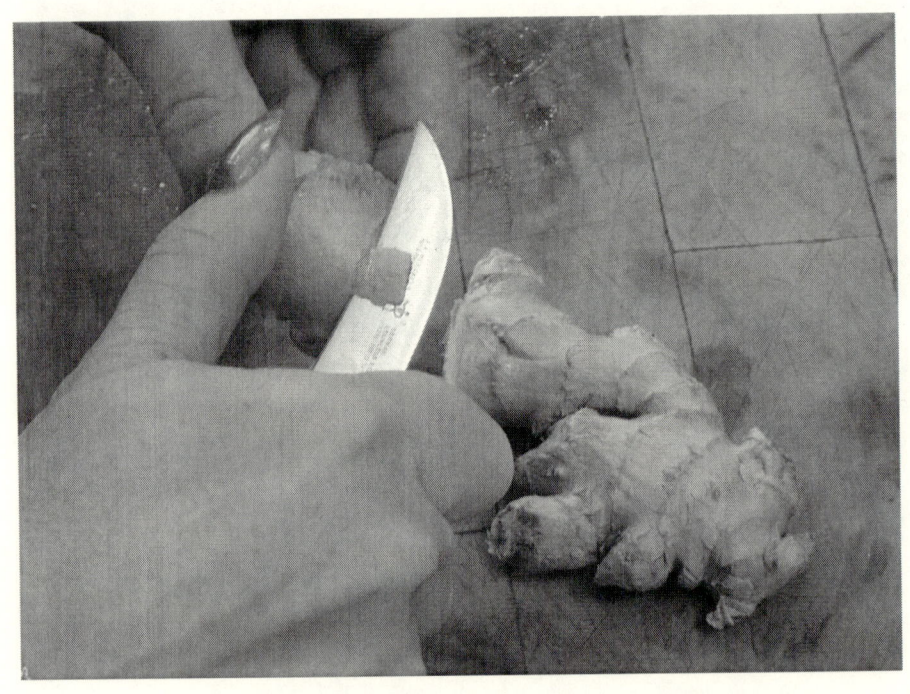

Use a sharp paring knife to peel fresh ginger

(you can also use the edge of a small spoon)

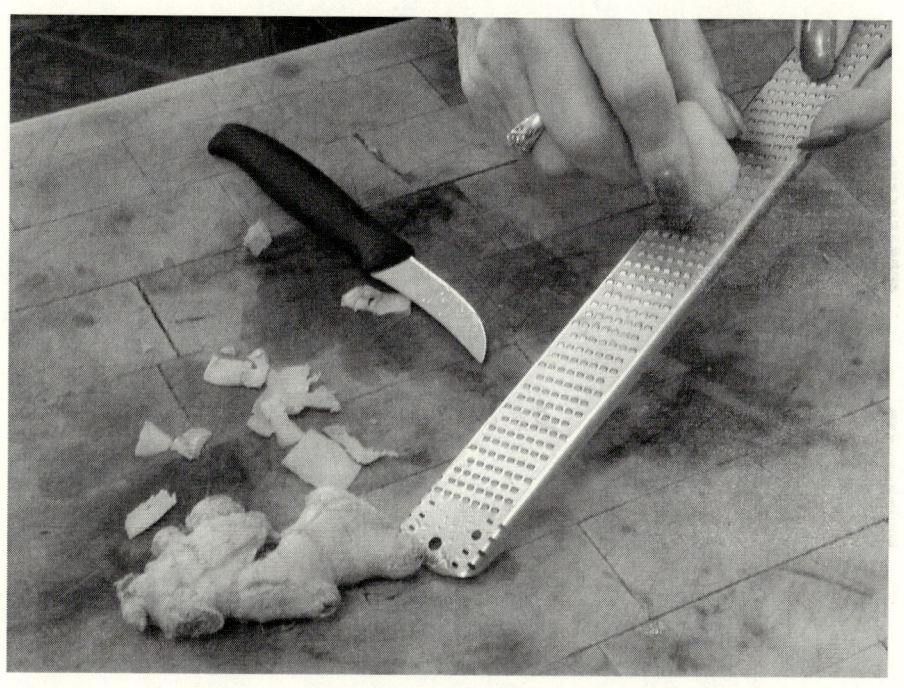

For finely grated ginger, use a metal rasp

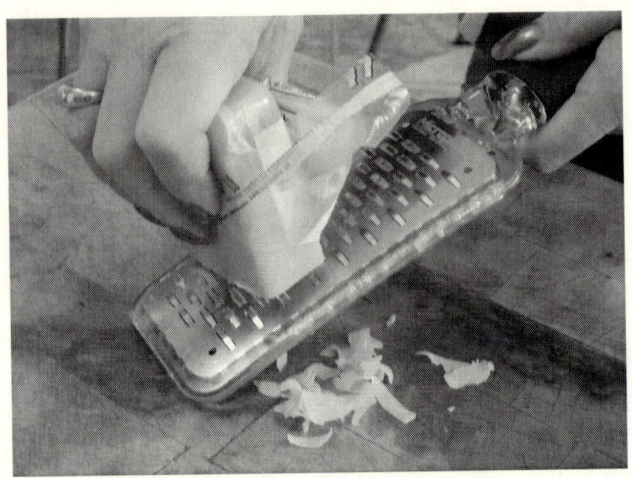

A Microplane will make grating hard cheeses easier

Stir Frying: (rear) metal wok with stirring ladle (front left to right) chili garlic sauce, sliced tofu, ginger (in bowl), hoisin sauce, chopped garlic (in bowl), soy sauce, diced green onion (Foreground) large chef's knife, plate of assorted vegetables, 2 eggs for fried rice, 1 cup dried rice (in bowl)

Cooking Tip: spray your pizza cutter with vegetable oil spray before using. It will be easier to clean.

* Instead of traditional tomato sauce, why not try basil pesto, garlic pesto or tapenade (olive spread). Use these sparingly; they will compliment the other flavors beautifully.

Crust:

Pita, Indian Nan bread or soft flour tortillas

Tomato Sauce*:
Use canned tomato sauce (Italian style), or pizza sauce. Add a little bottled salsa to the sauce for additional flavour

Seasonings (your choice):
Dried oregano, fresh basil, garlic powder, dried thyme, red pepper flakes

Toppings (choose 2 to 4):
Thinly sliced sweet or red onions, mushrooms, hot peppers, zucchini rings, blanched asparagus, canned artichokes, blanched broccoli, sweet red or green peppers, fresh garlic, green onions, tomato slices, black or green olives, sun-dried tomatoes, banana pepper rings, jalapeno peppers, Vegetarian pepperoni

Cheese:

Choose at least 2 different types—parmesan (fresh, grated), old cheddar, mozzarella, asiago, blue or feta (crumbled, small pieces)

Indian Spinach & Potato Balls with Spicy Yoghurt Sauce

You can tame the heat of the sauce by omitting the fresh ginger and hot peppers. This is an unusual dish. Serve with plain white rice.

10 minutes preparation
15 minutes cooking
4 servings

Mash the cooked potatoes in a large bowl together with the cooked drained spinach.

In a large non-stick sauté pan heat the oil on medium heat. When hot, add the cumin, and fry for 30 seconds. Add the onion and garlic and fry for 3 minutes. Add this mixture to the bowl containing the potato/spinach mixture. Add the coriander and Biryani sauce. Season with salt and pepper. Mix well to combine all the ingredients.

When the mixture is cool enough to handle, using your hands, form the mixture into 1" balls. Set aside. Using the same pan as before, add 3 tab vegetable oil. Heat on medium-high heat. When the oil is hot, add the balls and fry until browned (roll them over after a minute or two, and fry on all sides. It shouldn't take more than a few minutes). Remove the balls as they cook and drain them on paper towels. You may need to do several batches depending on the size of your pan.

When all the balls have been fried, prepare the sauce:

Put the yoghurt in a medium bowl. In a smaller bowl, put the ginger, garlic, hot green chili, cumin and coriander. Add a little water to make a paste. Heat the oil in a small sauté pan. Fry the onions for a few minutes until soft and add the spice paste. Fry on medium heat for a few minutes. Let cool at least five minutes. Stir this mixture into the bowl containing the yoghurt. Season with salt and pepper and lemon juice. Return the sauce to the small sauté pan and heat just enough to bring to a simmer (do not boil). Pour warmed sauce over the balls and serve at once.

Balls:

2 potatoes—peeled, boiled & mashed
½ package frozen, chopped spinach—cooked as package directs & drained

2 tab oil
1 teas ground cumin
¼ cup finely chopped sweet onion
1 clove minced garlic
2 tab chopped fresh coriander
1 generous tab Indian Biryani sauce*
salt & pepper to taste

3 tab vegetable oil

Sauce:
1-cup plain natural yoghurt
1 teas grated fresh ginger
1 clove minced garlic
1/2 long green chili pepper—finely minced
1 teas ground cumin
1 teas ground coriander seeds

2 tab oil

¼ cup chopped sweet onion
salt & pepper to taste
Squeeze fresh lemon juice to taste (start with the juice of a ¼ lemon and add the juice a ¼ lemon at a time, stirring well after each addition, until the sauce is to your liking)

*Biryani sauce is available in the grocery store in bottles or cans, in mild, medium or hot.

Moroccan Vegetable Stew

This is a very flavorful stew, easily prepared using the pressure cooker or stovetop.

Serve with couscous for an authentic dish. You could add a few golden raisins and/or cashews to the finished dish for even more flavor.

15 minutes preparation
35 minutes cooking or 3 minutes pressure cooker and 5 minutes simmer
4-6 servings

Sauté the onions and garlic in olive oil until the onions are tender, about 5 minutes. Add all the spices, lemon zest & juice, and all the vegetables. Simmer on low heat for 15 minutes until the vegetables (especially the carrots) are tender. Add the vegetable stock and olives. Cover and simmer an additional 10 minutes until all the vegetables are tender.* Add the chick peas and tomatoes and simmer another 5 minutes until the tomatoes have been incorporated. Sprinkle coriander on each serving.

* If using the pressure cooker, sauté the onions and garlic in olive oil until the onions are tender, about 5 minutes. Add all the other ingredients (including the vegetable stock) at the same time (except the chick peas and tomatoes) and bring the cooker to high pressure for 3 minutes. Carefully remove the lid and add the tomatoes and chickpeas. Reduce the heat to low and simmer (with the lid partly covering the cooker), for an additional 5 minutes.

Couscous:

In a medium saucepan on high heat, combine butter (if using) with vegetable stock. Bring to a boil. Remove the saucepan from the heat and quickly stir in the couscous. Cover immediately and let stand for five minutes. Stir in the mint and fluff with a fork.

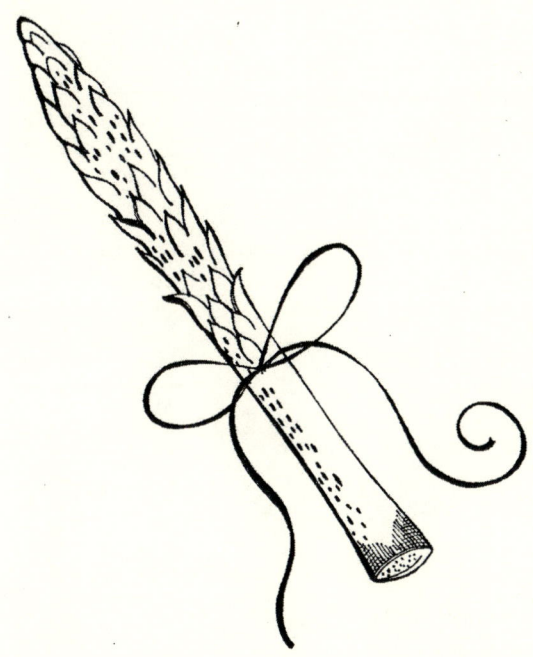

Food Fact: did you know that Couscous is actually a type of pasta? It originated in Northwest Africa and is made from semolina wheat, just like dried pasta!

2 tab olive oil
½ sweet onion, finely diced

5 green onions, thinly sliced on an angle
3 cloves garlic, finely chopped
½ teas ground coriander
¼ teas turmeric
1-2 crushed dried whole red chilies**
Salt & pepper to taste
2 teas ground cumin
1 teas cinnamon
Grated zest of 2 lemons
Juice from ½ lemon
2 stalks celery, diced***
½ small butternut squash****
½ sweet red or green pepper, diced
¼ cup diced green beans
2 carrots, peeled & finely diced

2 cups vegetable stock
¼ cup green salad olives, sliced (optional)

¼ cup canned chick peas
2 tomatoes, diced

Garnish:
3 tab finely chopped fresh coriander

Couscous:
1 tab butter (optional)
1 ¾ cup vegetable stock
1 cup couscous
¼ cup finely chopped fresh mint

**   Substitute 2-3 chopped hot banana pepper rings for more kick
***I always remove the "strings" from celery using a vegetable peeler
**** Try other varieties of squash including zucchini or pumpkin for a different flavor

Onion Tart

If you love onions, this is the pie for you! Serve hot or cold with a mixed green salad for a light, summer meal.

Individual slices make a great cold lunch the next day with a little chutney on the side.

10 minutes preparation
10-12 minutes baking (pie crust)
30 minutes baking (pie)
4 servings

Bake the pie shell as package directs. Put on a cooling rack and set aside until ready to use.

Pre-heat the oven to $375°$

In a large non-stick sauté pan, heat the oil on medium-low. Add the onions. Sprinkle the onions with balsamic vinegar and sauté slowly until the onions are completely browned and starting to caramelize, approx. 15 minutes. Using a slotted spoon, remove the onions from the pan and distribute them evenly over the bottom of the baked pie shell.

In a medium bowl, mix together the egg, cream and grated cheese. Season with salt, pepper and a little nutmeg.

Pour this mixture evenly over the onions in the pie shell.
Bake in a pre-heated $375°$ oven for approx. 30 minutes until the top of the pie feels firm.

LAUREEN OSBORNE

1 deep dish frozen pie shell, defrosted and baked as directed for a single pie crust

2 tab vegetable oil
2 lb bag cooking onions, peeled and finely chopped
1 tab balsamic vinegar

1 large egg, beaten
½ cup whipping cream or table cream
¼ cup grated mild or medium cheese

salt, pepper, and freshly grated nutmeg (1/8 teas should be enough)

Food fact: do onions make you cry? Try placing the onions in your freezer for 10-15 minutes before using. Then peel and chop as per usual.

If you don't have time to chill the onions, chop them near your sink and keep running your knife and the onion under the cold water. This rinses away some of the onion juice as you work.

Oriental Noodle Salad

This is a great summertime meal when you don't feel like heating up the kitchen and going to a lot of bother. Its great if you make it the night before so the vegetables can marinate overnight.

Vary the vegetables to your liking—try adding canned baby corn (steam as for cauliflower). bamboo shoots (right out of the can), or bean sprouts (steamed for 1-2 minutes). Drain all the vegetables well so they don't dilute your marinade.

10 minutes preparation
5 minutes steaming
2 hours chilling
4 servings as a main course

Wash all the vegetables. Steam both cauliflower and snow peas just until tender. (I usually put the cauliflower in a small sauce pan with enough water to barely cover. Bring the water to a boil and move the pieces in the boiling water for 3-5 minutes. Take a piece out and cool it under running cold water. Taste it and see if its cooked to your liking). Remove cauliflower from the sauce pan with tongs and put it in a large ceramic or plastic bowl along with the rest of the vegetables. Steam the snow peas in the same saucepan you just used and follow the same tasting process (they will cook quicker; probably in about 2-3 minutes).

Put all marinade ingredients in the blender and blend until smooth.

Pour the marinade over the vegetables in the bowl and add cooked soba noodles and toss to combine.

Cover the bowl and chill in the fridge for a couple of hours or overnight. Just before serving, toss again and sprinkle with sesame seeds and green onion.

½ medium head cauliflower—broken into bite-sized pieces
1 cup snow peas, prepared*
1 stick celery prepared**
½ English cucumber, partly peeled*** and cut into bite-sized pieces

Marinade:
2 tab Tamari soy sauce
½ teas garlic chili sauce
1 tab honey
1/3 cup vegetable stock
2 tab Tahini
1 tab rice wine vinegar
1 teas minced garlic
1 teas minced fresh ginger

1 ½ teas toasted sesame seeds
2-3 green onions, sliced on the diagonal

Soba noodles, Thai rice noodles or linguine—prepare 4 servings as the package directs, let cool.

*To prepare snow peas, wash them and cut the end off one tip with a paring knife. Don't cut all the way through and you will be able to peel a seam down one side of the snow pea. This will remove the tough fiber. Choose the larger of the two tips if you only want to seam on side.

**Using a peeler, remove the "strings" from the ribs and wash the stalk. Cut into bite sized pieces.
*** I use a peeler and remove 1" strips off the cucumber, leaving 1" strip of peel between each peeled strip. This makes the chunks more interesting to look at and you still get some of the nutrients found in the peel.

Roasted Vegetables with Pasta

10-minute preparation
20-30 minutes baking at 450°
Serves 4

Place the vegetables and garlic in a large roasting pan. Pour 2-3 tab olive oil over the vegetables to coat all the pieces. Sprinkle with balsamic vinegar and stir with a large spoon until all the vegetables are covered in oil and vinegar. Bake for 10 minutes. Stir again and bake another 10 minutes or more until the vegetables are cooked to your liking. (Whether you like them crunchy or soft).

While the vegetables are roasting, prepare the pasta as the package directs. Drain the cooked pasta. Place it in a large bowl, and add the roasted vegetables (and any liquid from the roasting pan), and stir to incorporate. Garnish with freshly grated Parmesan and basil, and season with salt & pepper.

Quick Tip: When in season, you can substitute fresh asparagus for the zucchini.

Cut the following vegetables into bite-sized pieces:
1 medium zucchini
1 sweet red or green pepper
1 lb fresh Italian plum tomatoes (3-4 medium size)
½ sweet onion
Olive oil
1-2 tab Balsamic vinegar
3 large cloves garlic—finely chopped

Garnish:
Parmesan (2-3 tab freshly grated)
Fresh basil (handful chopped leaves)

Cooked pasta shapes (penne, spirals, etc)
¼ cup olive or vegetable oil

Singapore Fried Vermicelli

This is another one of those easy stir fry dishes where you can add whatever vegetables you like; just make sure the pieces are small enough to pop in your mouth. You can substitute angel hair pasta or spaghettini if you don't have vermicelli noodles. If you're in a big hurry, steam the vegetables for a few minutes before adding them to the wok.

10 minutes preparation
20 minutes soaking vermicelli rice noodles or 12 minutes cooking pasta
15 minutes stir-frying
4 servings

Prepare vermicelli noodles as directed. When ready (or when your pasta is cooked), drain and rinse. Place cooked noodles in a bowl and pour vegetarian chicken stock over them and mix in. Let this mixture sit while you prepare the vegetables.

Heat the oil in your wok on high heat. When it reaches high temperature, add the onion and stir-fry. After a minute or two, add the garlic. Stir-fry for another 10 seconds. Add the chili pepper and stir-fry 10 seconds.

Add the prepared vegetables and stir fry the pieces until they're cooked to your liking (remove a piece of broccoli after five minutes and see if its cooked enough for you. If not, sprinkle the wok with a couple of tablespoons of water, put the lid on and steam for 1 minute).

When the vegetables are done, scrape them to the side of the wok and add 1 tab of oil to the bottom of the wok. Stir the curry powder and turmeric powder into the oil and cook for 10 seconds. Remove the wok from the heat. Lift the noodles out of the stock and drain them in a colander. Carefully (so you don't get splashed by hot oil), pour the stock into the spice mixture in the bottom of the wok. Return the wok to the heat and combine to make a sauce.

Quickly add the drained noodles to the wok, mixing them into the sauce. Put the noodles to the side of the wok where the vegetables are so you can add the eggs (Note: if the wok is getting too crowded to fit everything, remove the vegetables to a separate plate until the eggs are done, then add them back in and stir fry for 15 seconds until they are reheated). Put the beaten egg into the bottom of the wok and swish it around so it splashes up the sides a little. This will create a thinner layer and the egg will cook more evenly. When the eggs start to set, cut it into strips with your wok strainer and when all the egg is cooked, incorporate the egg into the noodles and vegetables to complete the dish. Garnish each serving with green onion and coriander.

Vermicelli noodles prepared as package directs 4 servings (then soak in vegetarian chicken stock)
½ cup vegetarian chicken stock

2 tab oil
½ sweet onion, finely diced
2 large clove garlic—finely minced
1 green chili pepper, finely minced (optional)

Assorted vegetables (1/2 cup each) cut in bite-sized pieces:
Broccoli
Bean sprouts
Chinese cabbage (Napa) or Bok Choy
carrots
peas

1 tab oil
1 tab mild curry powder
½ tab turmeric powder

LAUREEN OSBORNE

2 eggs, beaten

Garnish:
2 green onions, sliced diagonally
handful fresh coriander leaves, chopped

Spanakopita

This is an easier version of the Greek classic; this one is made with Fyllo pastry instead of pie crust. You can make these as individual servings or fold them into triangles. You can cut the triangles in half before baking, giving you smaller triangles. These small triangles are the perfect size for appetizers.

10 minutes preparation
20 minutes baking at 350°
6 servings

Pre-heat the oven to 350°

Combine spinach, leeks, feta and seasonings in a large bowl.

In a medium bowl, combine 2 beaten eggs with cornstarch. Add the egg mixture to the spinach mixture and combine well.

You can prepare the spanakopita as slices or turnovers. To make slices, place four sheets of fyllo (one sheet on top of another) onto a baking sheet that has been sprayed with vegetable spray. Spread the spinach mixture evenly over the sheets and top with four more sheets (using a pastry brush, moisten the edges of bottom sheet with egg "glue" so the top layer sticks to the bottom layer, and the filling doesn't leak). Bake 20 minutes until golden brown and crispy. After baking, let cool for five minutes and cut into six serving slices.

To make turnovers, place four sheets of fyllo (one sheet on top of another), onto a baking sheet that has been sprayed with vegetable spray.

Cut the stack into six equal squares. Put a spoonful of filling in the middle of each square and fold over the square on the diagonal to form a triangle. Use the egg "glue" to stick the top and bottom edges of each triangle together so the filling doesn't leak.

Bake 20 minutes until golden brown and crispy.

4 cups fresh spinach* or 2 packages frozen—thawed, drained and squeezed
2 leeks, finely chopped
1 cup feta cheese, crumbled
2 tab fresh dill
2 tab fresh basil
1 tab fresh lemon juice
salt & pepper to taste

2 eggs, beaten
1 teas cornstarch

1 package frozen fyllo pastry—thawed but kept moist (cover the sheets with a damp tea towel)

1 egg & 1 tab milk ("glue")

*If you feel adventurous, substitute finely chopped swiss chard or rapini instead of spinach. The flavor will be stronger. Use kitchen scissors and remove the tough middle rib from each leaf (you won't need to do this with smaller leaves)

Thai Curry Stew

Don't be intimidated by the number of ingredients—most of them get thrown in the blender. You can make a lot of substitutions for the vegetables. Try different varieties of squash or use fresh pumpkin. Try Yukon Gold (yellow-skinned) potatoes instead of sweet potatoes. You could also try using zucchini, cauliflower, or peas. You can also substitute other legumes for the chickpeas.

15 minutes preparation
30 minutes cooking
4 servings

Microwave the squash first. When its cool enough to handle, slice it in half, remove the seeds and "strings," remove the skin and chop the flesh into bite-sized pieces and set aside to add to the pot later.

Soak the tamarind in hot water and after 5 minutes, start to mash it with a fork to make a watery sauce. Mash again after 10 minutes and pour the contents of the bowl through a fine strainer and add this liquid to the blender. Discard the solids.

Simmer the vegetable stock in a Dutch oven or stockpot. Add the sweet potato, carrot, parsnip, red pepper and green beans and allow simmering 5-10 minutes while you prepare the curry sauce.

Add all curry sauce ingredients to the tamarind liquid already in the blender. Blend until smooth.

Pour the sauce over the vegetables in the Dutch oven. Add cooked squash, tomatoes, chickpeas and the orange rind. Simmer, covered on low heat for 15-20 minutes until all the vegetables are tender. While the stew simmers, prepare some Thai white rice to serve with it.

Sprinkle each serving with a garnish of your choice.

1 small butternut squash, pierced with a knife in several places and microwaved on high for 5-6 min.
1 cup vegetable stock
½ large sweet potato—peeled and cut into bite-sized pieces
1 large carrot—peeled and sliced
1 parsnip—peeled and sliced
¼ sweet red pepper—cut into bite-sized pieces
½ lb green beans—ends removed and cut into 1" pieces

1 cup cherry or grape tomatoes
½ can chickpeas—drained
2 tab grated orange rind

Curry Sauce:
3 medium cloves garlic—smashed
2 tsp Chinese garlic chili sauce
1 can unsweetened coconut milk
1" piece tamarind concentrate*—soaked in a bowl, with ¼ cup boiling water for 10 minutes
2 tab fish sauce or Marmite
juice of 1 lime
juice of 1 orange
½ teas turmeric powder
1 tab rice vinegar
1 tab each ground coriander, cumin
1 teas ground fennel
¼ mild sweet onion, roughly sliced

Garnish:

Fresh Thai basil leaves, chopped or fresh coriander leaves, chopped

*Tamarind is sold in vacuum sealed packages, available from Caribbean, Indian or Asian markets. If you can't find it, you can substitute the juice from ½ fresh lime.

Vegetable Curry

Accompany this dish with a serving of basmati rice, Raita and some mango chutney.

15-minute preparation
30 minute cooking (approx.)
4 servings

Toast the mustard, fennel, fenugreek, cumin and coriander seeds in a small non-stick frying pan. Heat over high until they begin to "pop" (this only takes a minute or two). Stir and immediately remove from the heat. Do not burn them!

Grind the seeds in a grinder. When ground, add the turmeric, cardamom, chili and peppercorns. Grind for 30 seconds so the spice mixture is incorporated. You have now made a "curry powder."

Heat the butter and oil in a medium sized non-stick sauté pan, over medium-low heat. Stir in the onion and the curry powder. Fry gently for 15 minutes. You have now made a "curry sauce." Remove from the heat.

While the curry is frying, wash the vegetables and chop them into bite-sized pieces. To decrease the cooking time, you can microwave each type of chopped vegetable in a small quantity of water in a microwave container for 2—3 minutes, just until tender. Drain off the water.

Add butter and oil to a large non-stick skillet over medium heat. Add the vegetables and sauté for about 5 minutes. Add the curry sauce and combine well. Sauté for another 2-3 minutes. Add the tomato juice and lemon juice and simmer, covered for approx 20 minutes (you will only need to simmer for approx 10 minutes if the vegetables have been micro waved). Season to taste with salt.

Like stew, this dish will improve if re-heated.

For a richer flavor, just before serving stir in two heaping tablespoons of natural yogurt and serve immediately.

Curry Powder:
2 teas mustard seeds, fennel seeds, fenugreek
1 tab each cumin seeds, coriander seeds
2 teas ground turmeric
¼ teas cardamom seeds (removed from the pods)
1 dried hot red chili
1 teas whole black peppercorn

2 tab butter, 2-tab oil
1 cup finely diced onion

4 cups of assorted vegetables:
Potatoes
Cauliflower
Green beans
Zucchini
Sweet peppers
Carrots
Peas

2 tab butter
1 tab oil
1 ½ to 2 cups tomato juice
Lemon juice to taste (start with juice from ¼ lemon)
salt to taste

2 tab natural yogurt (optional)

Vegetarian Stew

Eat this stew with mashed potatoes and you will feel the comforts of home. Keep your dice small so the pieces cook evenly and they will fit neatly in your mouth!

Keep the pot on a low simmer if you have the time, otherwise use your pressure cooker and eat in no time.

10 minute preparation
1 ½ hour simmer or 3 minutes (pressure cooker)
Serves 4

Heat the oil over medium-low heat in the bottom of a Dutch oven. Add the onions and garlic and fry gently. Lower the heat and add the fresh vegetables as you chop them, giving the pot a stir after each addition.

Add canned vegetables and lentils.

Using a large measuring cup (at least 3 cup capacity), place the vegetable stock powder in the bottom, then slowing add the water and stir until the stock has dissolved. In a separate small bowl, put the flour in the bottom and add a couple of tablespoons of the mixed stock. Stir until the flour and stock are combined. Add this mixture to the large measuring cup of stock. Add the onion soup mix to this and stir to combine. Pour the whole thing over your stew and bring to a boil. Reduce the heat, cover and simmer (stirring occasionally) for 1-1/2 hours or until all the vegetables are cooked to your liking.

VEGETARIAN FOR A DAY

1 pouch onion soup mix
3 cups boiling water
1 heaping teas. vegetable stock powder
2 tab flour
½ 28 oz. can whole tomatoes—roughly chopped

2 tab vegetable oil
½ sweet onion, diced
2 large cloves garlic, minced
2 teas Marmite©
generous splash Worcestershire sauce
2 medium carrots, diced
½ medium Chinese eggplant, diced
½ small zucchini, diced
1/8 th sweet red pepper, diced
3-4 mini potatoes—cut in half
½ small can peas
¼ small can baby corn—cut each corn in half lengthwise
½ can lentils, drained

Winter Vegetable Stew

Fall and winter root vegetables and squash can take a long time to cook. This recipe takes no time at all if you use a pressure cooker. Directions for stove top cooking follows the pressure cooker directions.

15-minute preparation
5 minute cooking (pressure cooker)
20 minutes cooking (stove top)
4-6 servings

Prepare all the vegetables. Put all the ingredients (except the couscous), into the pressure cooker. Cook under high pressure for 5 minutes. Remove from the heat and let sit for 5 minutes to allow the pressure to come down. Carefully release the pressure cooker lid and remove.

Put the couscous in a small bowl and rest the bowl on top of the cooked stew. Put the lid back on and lock. Leave 5 minutes until couscous is steamed and cooked.

Stove Top Method:

Sauté the onions and ginger in 2 tab of vegetable oil for a few minutes. Add the vegetables and sauté over low heat 20 minutes or until vegetables are cooked to desired doneness*. Add the rest of the ingredients (except the couscous) and simmer 10 minutes more to incorporate the flavors.

While the stew is simmering, prepare the couscous. Add the couscous to a small pot with a lid. Cook the couscous according to the package directions (usually in an equal quantity of water or stock).

*You can speed up the vegetable cooking time by pre-cooking them a few minutes in the microwave (place each type of vegetable in a microwave container in a small quantity of water, and microwave on high heat for 2-3 minutes until partially cooked).

1 teas minced fresh ginger
½ sweet onion, diced
2 tab vegetable oil (stove top cooking only)
1 small acorn or butternut squash, skin removed, seeds removed and chopped into bite-sized pieces
½ medium zucchini, diced
½ can tomato or vegetable cocktail juice
1 or 2 tab hot banana pepper rings (optional)
3 each: parsnips, carrots, peeled & diced
4 fresh tomatoes, seeded & diced

3-4 tab fresh coriander, finely chopped
½ fresh lime, juiced
½ 19 oz can fava or pinto beans
2 tab curry powder (or to taste)

1 cup couscous

Introduction to Tofu

By now, most people have at least tried tofu. Unfortunately, many have had a poor "first impression." Comments range from "tasteless," "boring" to "awful texture."

It's too bad that tofu has had a bad rap. The fact of the matter is, tofu will blend in to just about any conventional dish and will provide a nourishing boost.

Tofu is most commonly used in traditional eastern cooking such as Chinese or Thai. Stir fried or baked in a delicious sauce and you have a very fast meal on the table in no time. Once all your ingredients are chopped, your complete meal can be cooked in less than ten minutes—talk about "fast food"!

What the heck is "Tofu" anyway?

Tofu is made from soya beans. The beans are soaked in water. The water is saved—this is soya milk. The milk is then simmered and calcium sulphate or magnesium chloride [8] is added to help the milk coagulate into "curds." The curds are then pressed into a mould which squeezes the liquid out. The molded product is tofu.

Tofu is usually sold either in a container of water or is vacuum sealed. There are three different styles of tofu available on the market. My favorite is extra firm, but try all three. Each has a different recommended use:

Firm or extra firm—can be cubed for stir-frying, grilled or baked

Soft—is similar in consistency to scrambled eggs and can be blended into sauces

Silken—is most often used for puddings, sauces or dips

Why should you eat it?

Tofu is very high in protein and calcium and contains a chemical compound known as Isoflavones, which are thought to lower blood cholesterol and may prevent certain hormone-related cancers.

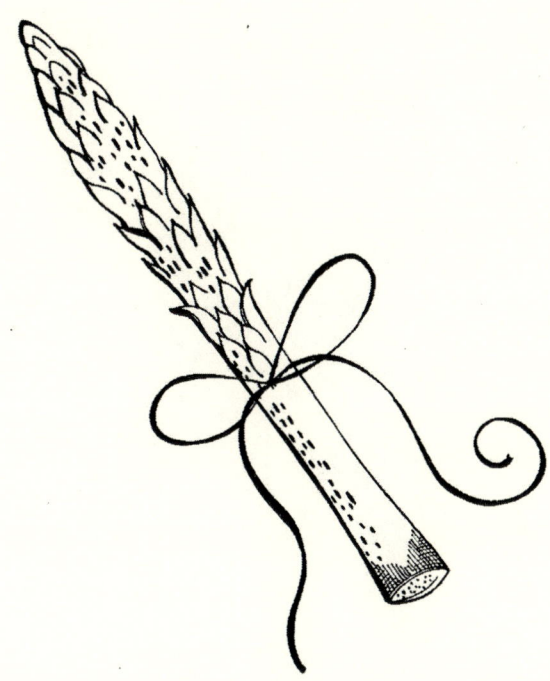

Food Fact: The Soybean is the only bean which contains all the amino acids needed to make a complete protein (all other beans should be consumed with grains, nuts and seeds).

Protein—half-cup (approx. 4 oz) serving of raw tofu contains 10.1 grams of protein (an egg contains 6 grams and 4 oz of ground beef contains about 26 grams of protein. Remember the RDA is 56 grams for most men and 46 grams for most women).

Calcium—half-cup serving of tofu contains 227 mg of calcium or about 22% of the RDA.

Stir Frying

This method of cooking originated in Asia. Stir frying is done using a Wok, which is a deep, round sauté pan. Woks are made from metal or aluminum, and have one or more handles on the sides to help you remove the wok from the heat. Stir frying is done on the stove top, either on an electric or gas element.

A wok is a good investment if you want to learn to cook meals **fast.** You can find them in department stores or from an oriental supermarket. Look for one that comes with a lid. Sometimes you can find them with a metal ring. This ring fits over the stove element, and the wok rests on the ring. You can place the wok directly on the stove element.

Sir frying cooks the pieces of food very fast because you are using high heat. The pieces don't burn because you keep them moving by constantly stirring everything around in the wok.

Use vegetable oil or peanut oil. It will heat without burning. Pour a couple of tablespoons into the bottom of the wok and place on high heat. After a few minutes the oil will begin to smoke. If you're not sure its hot enough, sprinkle one or two drops of water in the wok. It should sizzle. Be careful when adding your ingredients; the wok may be too hot and you could be splashed by the hot oil. Try to slip the ingredients down the side of the wok, rather than dumping them in from above.

The most important things to remember:

Have all your ingredients chopped and ready to go—once you start cooking, there is no stopping!

Have any sauces you plan to use already poured into small bowls (most store-bought sauces will go a little further if you dilute them with a little water)

Have your garnishes already chopped and placed on a small plate. *

Group all the ingredients for each dish together on a plate, along with the sauce for each dish. I usually prepare a tofu dish, a vegetable dish and some rice.

I prepare the tofu one of two ways; I either fry the tofu first in a small quantity of oil in the bottom of the wok. When browned, I remove it and drain the tofu on paper towels. I return it later to the wok when the vegetables are done along with the sauce, or I just add the tofu at the same time as the vegetables.

Steam your rice *first* so it has a chance to cool but fry the rice *last* as it will make a mess of your wok (the rice tends to stick a bit).

You will have to experiment a few times to find the right amount of cooking required for each type of vegetable. Some vegetables such as carrots and broccoli benefit from a few minutes of steaming. To steam them, add them to the heated wok first. Pour approx. ¼ cup of cold water over them and up the sides of the wok. Quickly place the lid on and let the vegetables steam for a minute or two. You can remove one piece and taste it to see if it has started to cook. You can then add the rest of the vegetables you will be using, and stir-fry as usual.

There is no limit to the variety of vegetables you can use, although I would not recommend starchy vegetables like potatoes. Here is a list of recommended vegetables to try:

    broccoli
    cauliflower
    snow peas
    green beans
    bamboo shoots
    water chestnuts
    carrots
    miniature corn
    bean sprouts
    zucchini
    onions
    mushrooms
    tomatoes
    asparagus

Try to cook the denser vegetables first, to give them a little extra time (or steam them as described above).

Stir Fry Sauce:
Here is my recipe. Use it as a starting point if you want to develop your own sauce:

2 tab soy sauce
2 tab hoisin sauce
1 teas chili garlic sauce
1 teas sugar
1" piece fresh ginger, peeled and grated
1 large clove garlic, finely chopped
½ cup vegetable stock
1 tab cornstarch stirred in a small bowl with 3 tab water, to make a white liquid

Mix together all the ingredients in a medium-sized bowl, except the cornstarch mixture. When the stir-fried vegetables (and tofu) are cooked to your liking, make an opening "well" in the center of your wok by pushing the cooked vegetables up the sides of your wok. Add the sauce to the well and heat to boiling. Quickly stir the cornstarch mixture into the sauce. As the sauce starts to thicken, incorporate the vegetables so that each vegetable gets a little sauce on it. Quickly remove from the heat and serve, garnished as desired.

* Here is a list of garnishes to try:

sliced green onion "scallions"
"matchstick" sliced cucumber or carrot
chopped peanuts, pumpkin seeds or cashews
toasted sesame seeds
bean sprouts
finely sliced sweet red or green pepper
Chopped fresh coriander or Thai basil

Tofu: Recipes

Baked Tofu

Sliced, baked tofu is very handy to have on hand. It can be cubed and added to a stir fry or cold noodle salad* or Tofu Satay**. Slices can be added to a wrap along with bean sprouts and grilled vegetables for a tasty picnic lunch.

5 minutes preparation
30 minutes marinating
25 minutes baking at 450°

Mix marinade ingredients together in a large glass baking dish. Add tofu pieces and turn to coat evenly with marinade. Cover with plastic wrap and marinate 30 minutes, turning the tofu a few times if you remember.

Remove the plastic wrap and bake the tofu in a 450° oven for 7 minutes. Using tongs, carefully turn each piece of tofu over and bake 8 minutes longer. Remove from it from the oven and add the sauce.

To make the sauce, combine the sauce ingredients in a small bowl. Brush the tofu pieces on both sides with the sauce. Put the tofu pieces back in the oven and bake 8 to 10 minutes more, just until the tofu turns golden brown.

*For cold noodle salad—make a double recipe of marinade, and add 2 tab of fresh lemon juice and 1 tab toasted sesame seeds. Combine these ingredients in a large salad bowl along with cooked noodles, blanched vegetables such as asparagus, snow peas and green beans. Top with slivers of sweet red pepper, cucumber sticks and two tab fresh finely chopped coriander. Add ½ a recipe of baked tofu which has been cut into

1" cubes. Combine well and refrigerate covered, for a few hours (or overnight) to let the flavors develop. A couple of times during refrigeration give the mixture a stir to ensure all the ingredients are coated with the marinade.

** For Tofu Satay—Cube the tofu slightly larger than 1" so they will safely stay on bamboo skewers. For appetizers, alternate one grape tomato with one cube of tofu to fill the skewer. Place on a hot grill and grill 2 minutes per side. Serve with Satay Sauce: mix together in a small bowl

1 tab olive oil, 2 tab sesame oil, 1" piece finely grated peeled ginger, 1 teas chili garlic sauce, 1 tab soy sauce and 1 tab smooth or chunky peanut butter.

Marinade:
2 tab tamari soy sauce
2 tab sesame oil
1" piece fresh ginger, peeled and finely grated

1 lb extra firm tofu cut in half lengthwise then each half placed on its side and cut in three, giving you 6 pieces total

Sauce:
1 teas garlic chili sauce
1 tab tahini
2 tab rice wine vinegar or orange juice

Noodle Soup

Once you've got your soup base, you can add just about any combination of suitable vegetables. As with stir frying, its best to chop the vegetables to a uniform size so they will cook evenly.

This soup is a meal in itself and is ready to serve very quickly. I usually prepare the base, start it simmering, and add the vegetables as I chop them. Omit the grated ginger and garlic chili sauce if you don't like spicy food.

15 minutes preparation
10 minutes cooking
4 servings

Boil the noodles as the package directs. Set them aside (keep them in their cooking water until they are ready to serve).

Drain the tofu. Wrap it in paper towel and press the water out by placing the tofu under a heavy pot or your toaster for 10 minutes if possible.

Place the dried mushrooms in a medium bowl. Pour boiling water over them just to cover. Let sit at least 10 minutes to allow them to re-hydrate. Save the water they are soaking in—it will be added to the soup.

In a large soup pot, add ginger, lemon grass, vegetarian stock, garlic chili sauce, lime juice, soaked mushrooms and their liquid, sesame oil, tamari soy sauce, and the fish sauce. Bring this to a boil then reduce the heat to a simmer.

Peel and uniformly dice the vegetables into bite-sized pieces. Add them to the soup pot as you prepare them. I usually add the densest vegetables (such as carrots) first to allow them extra cooking time. If you're really rushed, you can microwave the denser vegetables for two minutes (place diced vegetables in a microwavable container, add a small quantity of water, and microwave on high).

When you've added all the vegetables, give the pot a stir and make sure it is simmering. Slice the tofu into pieces, (2" long by ¼" wide by 1/8" thick), and add to the soup. Cover the pot slightly and simmer about ten minutes. Taste a spoonful and see if the vegetables are done to your liking.

Just before serving, sprinkle the pot with the freshly chopped coriander and basil.

Drain the noodles. Place one serving of noodles in the bottom of a deep soup bowl. Ladle the soup into the bowl and garnish as desired.

½ package Thai Rice Noodles (prepare separately—as package directs)

½ package organic extra firm tofu—cut the block of tofu in half lengthwise

¼ cup dried Chinese mushrooms

1 tab. freshly grated ginger
1 stick of lemon grass, cut in 1" pieces and flattened with a meat tenderizer
2 cups vegetarian beef or chicken stock
1 tab garlic chili sauce
juice of one lime
1 teas sesame oil
1 teas tamari soy sauce
2 tab fish sauce**

assorted vegetables (about 2 cups total): baby corn, baby or regular bok choi, carrots, snow peas, celery*

coriander 2 tab fresh chopped
Basil 4 large leaves fresh chopped

Garnish (optional):
sliced green onion, and/or thinly sliced strips of sweet red pepper

* You could also use broccoli, cauliflower, peas, bamboo shoots, leeks, Chinese cabbage, water chestnuts, asparagus

** Fish sauce gives this soup a uniquely Thai flavor. Vegetarians substitute 1 teas of Marmite

Spicy Bean Curd

Tofu is often referred to as "Bean Curd" in Asian restaurants. Go easy on the garlic chill sauce if you have youngsters trying this dish. Choose Hoisin over Black Bean sauce if you want the dish to be sweet.

Serve this spicy dish with plain steamed white rice. You can steam a green vegetable to serve on the side (such as asparagus, snow peas or green beans).

10 minutes preparation
15 minutes frying & stir frying
4 servings

In a small bowl, combine the sauce ingredients and set aside.

In another small bowl, combine the cornstarch and water to make a paste and set aside.

Prepare the tofu: Pour enough oil into the bottom of your wok to make a small pool (you will probably need 2 tablespoons). Pre-heat your wok over high heat. When the oil is hot, use your long handled tongs to gently slip pieces of tofu into the hot oil. Only add enough slices so that the pieces are not overlapping. Fry until golden brown (approx. 30 sec). Using your tongs, quickly flip the pieces over and fry the other side. Quickly remove the fried pieces to paper towel to drain.

When all the pieces are fried, pour off the excess oil. Lower the heat to medium high and add the garlic and ginger and stir-fry for 10 seconds. Stir in the sauce mixture and heat to boiling.

Add the fried tofu and stir fry to coat. Push the pieces of tofu up the sides of the wok and quickly stir in the cornstarch mixture to the sauce in the bottom of the wok. Stir-fry briskly until the sauce just starts to thicken. Stir the tofu pieces back into the thickened sauce and remove the wok from the heat. Serve immediately; garnish each serving with sesame seeds and green onions.

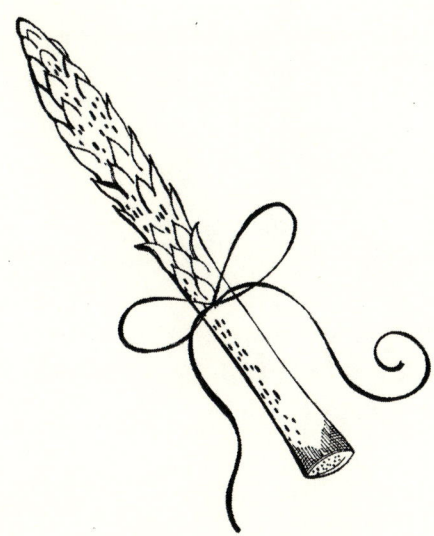

Cooking Tip: When you're trying to measure "sticky" ingredients like Hoisin sauce, peanut butter or honey, spray your measuring spoon or cup with cooking spray first—the ingredient will pour out easily!

Sauce ingredients:
1 tablespoon Garlic Chili Sauce
1 tablespoon Hoisin or Black Bean sauce ¼ cup vegetable stock
2 tablespoons tamari soy sauce

In an egg cup, mix together:
1 heaping tablespoon cornstarch
1 tablespoon water

1/2 lb firm tofu, drained and cut: to use ½ lb tofu, slice the tofu in half lengthwise. Take one piece and slice it into 3 lengths. Turn the lengths sideways, and cut into ¼" strips. This will give you pieces that are approx. 1" diameter and ¼" thick.

2 tab vegetable or peanut oil for the wok

1" piece fresh ginger—peeled and grated
1 large clove garlic—peeled and grated

Garnish:

1 Tab toasted sesame seeds*
2 green onions, sliced on the diagonal

*To toast seeds, place in a small, dry non-stick sauté pan. Heat on high. Slide the pan back and forth until the seeds start to brown. Immediately remove from the heat so they don't burn.

Tofu Loaf

This is a great dish to take along to a potluck or buffet dinner as it will serve a lot of people. I eat this at Christmas as the ingredients are reminiscent of turkey stuffing.

Preparation Time: 10 minutes
Cooking Time: 45 minutes
8-10 servings

Rinse, drain and dry the tofu. Put the tofu, bouillon cubes, arrowroot, agar powder and poultry seasoning into a food processor (I usually divide the mixture in half as it is almost too much capacity for my processor). Process until blended.

Spray a loaf tin with cooking spray. Line the bottom and sides of the pan with about half of the tofu mixture. The bottom and sides should be about a ½" thickness.

Mix the sautéed mushrooms into the prepared stuffing. Add the stuffing to the loaf tin and press it into the tofu. Cover the stuffing with the rest of the tofu and press firmly down.

Cover the loaf tin with tin foil and bake for 45 minutes at 350^0.

Remove the loaf from the oven and let cool at least 10 minutes before cutting into ½" slices. Pour the prepared gravy on each serving.

2 450 gr. packages extra firm tofu, dried
2 vegetable bouillon cubes, dissolved in 2 tbsp boiling water

4 tbsp arrowroot or cornstarch
1 tbsp agar powder *
1 tsp. poultry seasoning
¾ teas garlic powder

2 packages pre-mix stuffing—prepared as package directs**
½ cup of diced mushrooms that have been sautéed in 1 tab butter
2 packages chicken gravy mix ***

*Agar powder is made from a type of seaweed and is a jelling agent. If you can't find it, substitute gelatin (gelatin is NOT vegetarian as it is made from animals)
   ** Look for vegetarian
   *** Look for vegetarian

Tofu with Ginger Sauce

You can buy ready-made oriental sauces if its more convenient. Just simmer the sauce in a small saucepan while you prepare the tofu. This dish is best served with plain white rice and a side dish of oriental vegetables, which can quickly be prepared after you've fried the tofu. Simply pour off most of the oil and stir fry your veggies until done. Or you can also go "super simple" and serve the tofu with fresh bean sprouts and sliced green onions sprinkled on the top, instead of stir-fried vegetables.

5 minutes preparation
5 minutes cooking (ginger sauce)
15 minutes frying (tofu)

In a small non-stick saucepan, use a wooden spoon to combine the vinegar, sugar, water and soy sauce. Bring to a boil and reduce the heat to simmer for a few minutes. Stir in the grated ginger. In a small bowl, combine the cornstarch with a little water to make a paste and add to the sauce. Quickly stir until the sauce thickens. Remove from the heat and set aside.

When the sauce is ready, combine the egg, milk and Tabasco in a small bowl. In a separate bowl combine the flour, salt, pepper and garlic powder.

Pour enough vegetable oil into the wok to create a small well in the bottom. Heat the oil on high heat. Immediately dip each cube of tofu into the egg/milk mixture, then dip into the flour mixture so that the cube is coated. Immediately place the cube into the hot oil (use your long handled tongs for this so that you don't get splashed by the hot oil). Work quickly until the bottom of the well is covered in cubes. Allow the cubes to fry for 30 sec until golden brown, then gently turn them over and fry the other side. Immediately remove each cube and place it on a paper towel to drain. Repeat with the remaining cubes until all the pieces are fried.

When ready to serve, divide the tofu evenly among four plates and pour the reserved sauce over each serving. Sprinkle with sesame seeds.

Alternatively, you can serve the sauce separately in small bowls, one for each person. Each person can dip into their sauce as they eat a cube of tofu.

Ginger Sauce:

6 tab white vinegar
4 tab sugar
¾ cup water
2 tab dark soy sauce
1" fresh ginger—peeled and finely grated
1 tab cornstarch and 2 tab water

1 egg, beaten with 1 tab milk
A couple of drops of Tabasco sauce (optional)

2 tab flour
¼ teas salt
¼ teas pepper
¼ teas garlic powder

2 tab vegetable oil for the wok
½ lb extra firm tofu—dried and cut into 1" cubes

Garnish (optional):
1 tab toasted sesame seeds

Introduction to Pasta

When you want a quick, easy and nutritious meal, pasta is the answer. A dish of pasta and a salad or freshly steamed vegetables, is a great solution for those nights when you get home late and you want a quick meal.

Pasta is high in *complex* carbohydrates, which give you energy over a longer period of time compared to *simple* carbohydrates.

Dry pasta is made from hard wheat and is high in protein; fresh pasta is made from soft wheat and is less high in protein and may not be made with enriched flour.

In the United States and Canada, all dried pasta is made with enriched flour fortified with folic acid, an important B vitamin.

Here are a few tips for preparing pasta:

Start boiling the pasta *before* preparing your sauce as most of the sauce recipes will be ready before than the pasta

Add salt to your pasta boiling water

Do **not** add oil to your pasta boiling water; your sauce won't stick to the pasta

Save a little of the pasta boiling water to help thicken your sauce (the water contains a little starch from the pasta)

Break long pasta (such as spaghetti or linguine) in half before adding to the pot; it will cook more evenly

Use a large pot and a lot of water so that you can keep your pasta moving in the pot; stir it every few minutes so that it cooks evenly

Keep your oven and racks clean by baking pasta dishes (such as lasagna, ravioli, etc), on a non-stick cookie sheet (if you don't have a non-stick sheet, cover your baking sheet with a piece of parchment paper that has been cut to fit). If the cheese or sauce bubbles over, it will be easier to clean.

LAUREEN OSBORNE

Let baked dishes (such as lasagna) cool for about 15 minutes before trying to cut. The filling will be less runny and easier to cut into individual portions

Pasta: Recipes

Arrabiata Sauce

This sauce is spicy. If you don't like it too hot, eliminate the banana pepper rings and Chinese chili sauce.

10 minute preparation
15 minute cooking
4 servings

Saute onions, mushrooms and garlic in oil for 5 minutes until the vegetables are soft. Add the tomatoes and the remaining ingredients. Simmer for 15 minutes. Remove bay leaves and discard.

Serve over cooked pasta.

Quick Tip: If you want a thicker sauce, do not use all the liquid from the canned tomatoes and simmer the sauce an additional 15 minutes until the sauce reduces to the consistency you like.

½ Spanish onion, chopped
¼ cup fresh mushrooms, sliced
2 large cloves garlic, minced
¼ cup olive or vegetable oil
1 28 oz can diced Italian tomatoes, and their liquid
½ cup medium or mild bottled Salsa
2 generous tab pickled banana pepper rings, chopped
2 bay leaves
2 teas chili powder
½ teas dried crushed chilies
½ teas Chinese chili sauce
¼ cup olive or vegetable oil

Asian Noodle Salad

This is an easy to prepare cold salad, great with grilled chicken or fish (for the meat eaters in the family!)

20 minutes preparation
4 servings

Prepare the noodles as the package directs. Drain the noodles and set aside to cool. Blanch the broccoli and baby corn (to blanch, place the vegetables in a medium size saucepan. Add just enough boiling water to barely cover them. Place on high heat and boil for 2-3 minutes, just until the vegetables are starting to soften). Add the cooled noodles and the rest of the ingredients to a large bowl.

Whisk the dressing ingredients together in a small bowl and pour over the noodle mixture in the large bowl. Combine all the ingredients together so that everything has dressing on it.

Garnish the salad with finely chopped fresh coriander. Cover and refrigerate 1 hour to allow the flavors to develop.

Quick Tip: You can substitute the red pepper, cucumber and tomato with bean sprouts, snow peas and asparagus for a truly Asian flavor. Blanch the snow peas and asparagus before adding.

Food Fact: Tomatoes are a good source of lycopene, a phytochemical that has antioxidant properties. Antioxidant levels rise significantly when tomatoes are heated.

½ package Thai Noodles
½ head broccoli—flowerets only, cut into bite-size pieces
½ can baby corn
1 tab toasted sesame seeds
2 green onions, 1" pieces, sliced
¼ sweet red pepper, julienne
½ English cucumber, julienne
1 tomato cored & diced

Dressing:
2 tab Tamari soy sauce
1 Tab sesame oil
a few drops of Tabasco sauce
Juice of one lemon
1 tab fish sauce
½ tab sugar

Garnish:
2-3 tab Fresh coriander, roughly chopped

Broccoli Sauce

This is a very quick sauce to make so be sure and cook your pasta first.

A few drops of hot sauce or one dried red chil can be added to the pan of cooking broccoli for a bit of a "kick."

10-12 minute cooking (pasta)
10-minute cooking (sauce)
4 servings

Cook the pasta as the package directs and drain off the excess water.

Blanch the broccoli 2-5 minutes until its cooked to your liking. Heat the oil and butter in a large non-stick sauté pan over med-low heat. When the butter melts, add the garlic, and stir a few times. Sauté for 30 seconds. Add the broccoli, lemon zest and lemon juice. Sauté a couple of minutes until the broccoli is coated with the other ingredients in the pan.

Place the drained pasta in a large bowl and gently mix in the broccoli mixture. Gently stir in the Parmesan and basil to taste. Serve immediately. Use a large spoon for serving so that you can spoon up any sauce that may have fallen to the bottom of the bowl.

½ head of broccoli—flowerets only (no stems), cut into bite sized pieces

2 tab olive oil
2 tab butter
3 cloves minced garlic

LAUREEN OSBORNE

Zest and juice of one lemon

Salt & pepper to taste
Cooked pasta shapes such as shells, rigatoni, penne, etc.

Fresh Parmesan (approx. 2 tab, freshly grated)
5-6 large basil leaves, chiffonier

Coriander Sauce

For a low-fat version of this rich sauce, you can substitute low fat cream cheese for the regular cream cheese and substitute milk for the cream.

10 minutes preparation
10 minutes cooking
2—4 servings

Wash the coriander thoroughly and pat dry with paper towels. Remove the leaves from the larger, main stems and chop the leaves finely (discard the stems). Put the coriander leaves and pine nuts in a food processor and process into a paste.

Heat the oil in a large non-stick sauté pan over medium heat. Add the onions and sauté for a few minutes until tender. Add the coriander paste, cream cheese and cream. Reduce the heat to low and simmer for a few minutes until the cheese melts. Taste the sauce and season with salt & pepper. Add the cooked pasta and stir in to coat the pasta thoroughly. Serve immediately.

1 bunch fresh coriander
2 oz toasted pine nuts*

2 tab olive or vegetable oil
4 oz chopped green onions

1 250 gr package cream cheese, softened
4 oz half & half cream
Salt & pepper to taste

Cooked and drained pasta shapes such as penne, bows, rigatoni, etc.

*To toast, place in a medium sized dry, non-stick saucepan and heat over medium-high heat for approx. five minutes. Shake the pan (or stir the nuts), every 20 seconds so they don't burn. Remove from the heat as soon as they are golden brown on all sides. Remove from the pan to stop them from toasting any further.

Dill Sauce

You can use any mildly flavored bean for this dish. Eggs and dill work really well together—one or two chopped hard boiled eggs sprinkled on top of your finished dish will boost the protein level (not to mention the taste!)

10 minute preparation
10 minutes cooking
4 servings

Prepare the pasta as the package directs. Drain the cooked pasta and set aside.

Add the oil to a large non-stick sauté pan and heat over medium-high heat. Sauté the onions and garlic in the oil for a few minutes until the onions start to soften. Stir in the beans and the lemon juice. Reduce the heat slightly.

In a small bowl, whisk together the stock and the flour. Add this mixture to the pan of beans and stir a few times until the liquid in the pan starts to thicken slightly. Stir in the dill and the cooked pasta. Taste, and season with salt and pepper.

Divide the pasta between individual serving plates and garnish each with olives and green onion. Serve immediately.

Quick Tip: For a variation, add 2 chopped sundried tomatoes when you add the dill.

2 tab olive or vegetable oil

¼ cup diced sweet onion
1 large clove crushed garlic
1 ½ cans white kidney beans, navy beans or garbanzo beans, drained and rinsed
2 tab fresh lemon juice

1 cup vegetable stock
2 teas flour
¼ cup chopped fresh dill
salt and black pepper to taste

Garnish (optional):
¼ cup sliced black or green olives
2 chopped green onions

Fettuccine Alfredo

The perfect way to prepare a smooth sauce is to stir constantly over medium to low heat

10 minutes cooking
10 minutes boiling pasta (as package directs)
4 servings

In a small non-stick sauté pan, lightly fry the tomato and garlic in the olive oil over medium heat for a few minutes. Sprinkle with the basil, season with a little salt and set aside.

Heat the butter in a large non-stick sauté pan over medium heat. Add the flour and stir to incorporate. Sauté for 1 minute. Slowly stir in the cream and heat until the cream starts to steam. Add the bay leaf. Slowly stir in the parmesan a little at a time until the sauce starts to thicken and all the cheese has been added. Season with salt, pepper and a little freshly-grated nutmeg.

Add the cooked pasta to the Alfredo sauce, and stir to combine. Divide the pasta evenly between 4 individual plates. Place a serving of the tomato mixture in the centre of each dish of pasta. Pass an additional bowl of grated parmesan to be sprinkled on top, if desired.

1 medium tomato, chopped
1 large clove garlic, minced
4-6 basil leaves, chiffonade*

2 tab flour
2 tab butter
1 small carton 18% cream
1 bay leaf
½ cup or more grated Parmesan
nutmeg, salt & pepper to taste

4 servings fettuccini or penne pasta, cooked

Garnish:
Additional grating of Parmesan

*Quick Tip: Lay the basil leaves on top of each other, going from largest leaf to smallest. Roll them up lengthwise, cigar-style. When tightly rolled, finely slice using a sharp knife. You will be left with slivers or "chiffonade"

Fresh Tomato Sauce

This is about as simple (and fast) as it gets. This is a great sauce for the end of summer when your garden is full of beautiful, ripe red tomatoes. Start boiling the water for your pasta before you start this dish so that the pasta is ready by the time the sauce is finished.

Freshly steamed asparagus or green beans are a nice accompaniment to this dish.

10 minutes preparation
10 minutes cooking

Prepare the fresh tomatoes as directed below. Set aside.

Pour enough vegetable oil into the bottom of a large non-stick sauté pan to coat. Add the onions and fry gently over medium low heat until they begin to soften. When they are translucent (without being fried), stir in the garlic and sauté another minute.

Add the chopped tomatoes and their juice. Add salt, pepper and sugar*. Increase the heat slightly so the mixture starts to bubble and the tomato pieces start to break up.

At this point you can add 1 tablespoon of the water from the pasta that you are cooking and/or 1 heaping tablespoon of tomato paste. Both these items will help your sauce thicken. Keep the lid off and continue to cook another 5-7 minutes until the sauce thickens by evaporation of the tomato juices. Taste, and season with salt and pepper.

Just before serving, sprinkle with the freshly prepared basil and stir gently.

Top each plate with crumbled feta (optional).

Approx. 2 lbs vine ripe tomatoes*—prepared and chopped
2 tab vegetable oil
¼ to ½ mild sweet onion, finely diced
1 or 2 cloves garlic smashed, chopped

salt & pepper to taste
½ teas sugar**
1 tablespoon cooking water or tomato paste (optional)

handful fresh basil leaves, chiffonade

Garnish (optional):
Crumbled feta (approx. 1 once) for garnish

*To prepare tomatoes: Using a sharp knife, score the base of the tomato with a small "x"—just cut through the skin. This will prevent the tomato from bursting when it starts to boil. Place tomatoes in a large pot of rapidly boiling water for a few minutes until you can see the skin starting to peel back from the little "x" you made. Using long handles tongs, Immediately remove the tomatoes from the water and immerse them in a large bowl of ice water. They should now peel very easily.
Once peeled, squeeze each tomato over an empty bowl to remove the seeds. Discard the seeds. Core each tomato then chop the tomato into bite-size pieces. Save in a separate bowl along with any accumulated juices.

**Sugar is added to balance the acidity of the tomatoes. Tomatoes vary in acidity.

Lasagna with "Meat" Filling

This is a very substantial Lasagna so when you serve it, keep the portions small.

A lasagna dish measuring approx. 10" x 6" x 2" will make four servings. If you want to make a large pan of lasagna for a group, the recipe can be doubled. Cook the entire box of noodles, and use a lasagna dish measuring approx. 13" x 9" x 2."

10 minutes preparation
10-12 minutes cooking pasta (as package directs)
10 minutes cooking
30-40 minutes baking at 350º
4 servings

Pre-heat the oven to 350º Spray the lasagna dish with vegetable cooking spray (include any lip or handles in case the lasagna bubbles over). Cover the bottom of the dish with a thin layer of tomato sauce and set aside.

Boil the noodles and drain them in a colander. Rinse with cold water. Dry each noodle with paper towel and lay each side by side on a large piece of waxed paper. Make sure the noodles don't over lap or they will stick together.

Food Fact: tomatoes are rated #1 among fruits and vegetables as a source of vitamins and minerals in our diet. They are #1 because we eat so many of them!

In a large non-stick sauté pan, heat the oil on medium low heat. Add the onions and sauté a few minutes until they start to soften. Stir in the garlic. Sauté for one minute. Stir in the mushrooms and sauté for a few minutes until they begin to soften. Add the "veggie" ground round and stir to combine. Remove from the heat and stir in the hot peppers, olives and basil.

Put three lasagna noodles, lengthwise and side by side in the lasagna dish, on top of the sauce. Spread the noodles with half of the ground round mixture. Add three more noodles. Spread the noodles with the remaining ground round mixture. Top with the remaining three noodles.

Completely cover the top layer of noodles with the remaining sauce. Sprinkle the sauce with red pepper flakes and oregano. Top with grated cheddar and fill in any spaces with the Parmesan.

Place the lasagna dish on a baking sheet on the middle rack of the oven. Bake for 30-40 minutes until the lasagna is bubbling and the cheese(s) have melted.

Cool at least 15 minutes before cutting into servings.

½ box lasagna noodles (9 noodles) prepared as package directs

1 bottle or can (680 mls/approx. 23 oz. U.S.) roasted red pepper pasta sauce (or any flavor of tomato pasta sauce you prefer)
2-3 tab vegetable oil
½ mild sweet onion (such as Spanish or Vidalia), finely diced
1-2 large cloves garlic, smashed and minced
1 cup wild mushrooms*, finely diced
½ package "veggie" ground round"(Italian style if available)
1-2 tab pickled banana pepper rings, diced** (optional)
5-6 whole black olives, pitted and chopped
handful fresh basil leaves, chiffonade

½ teas each dried red pepper flakes, dried oregano
1 cup grated medium cheddar
¼ cup freshly grated Parmesan

* Choose an assortment of shitake, oyster, portobello or cremini (you can find mixed packages in most supermarkets)
 **Use the lesser amount if you're not sure how spicy you want it

Macaroni and Cheese

This is a sophisticated version of the family favorite.

10 minutes preparation
30-40 minutes baking at 350°
4-6 servings

Melt the butter in a large non-stick sauté pan. Add the flour and stir for one minute until the flour is blended. Slowly whisk in the milk. Whisk until the sauce thickens slightly. Add the cheeses and stir until incorporated into the sauce. Taste, and season with salt, pepper and a grating of nutmeg, if desired.

Combine the sauce with the macaroni and pour into a large baking dish that has been sprayed with non-stick vegetable spray. Top with crouton crumbs. Sprinkle with paprika. Bake 30 to 40 minutes until bubbling.

Variation: substitute cheddar for Swiss. Add a dash of Worcestershire and 1 teas Dijon mustard to the sauce when cooking.

½ stick butter
¼ cup flour
2 ½ cups milk
2 oz Gorgonzola cheese, crumbled
4 oz Gruyere or Emmentaler or other mild Swiss cheese
½ cup grated Parmesan
salt & pepper & nutmeg to taste

Macaroni—cooked and drained

¼ cup garlic croutons,
1/8 teas ground paprika

Marinara Sauce

Vegetarian pasta sauces have the advantage over meat sauces as they take very little time to cook. While the sauce is simmering and your pasta is boiling, prepare a tasty salad. You can have a quick, vegetarian pasta dish on the table in 20 minutes!

5 minutes preparation
15 minutes cooking
4 servings

Brown the onion and garlic in the oil, in the bottom of a large, heavy saucepan. This should take a couple of minutes on medium-high heat. Add the tomatoes and the remaining ingredients (except the basil). Season to taste with salt & pepper. Simmer the sauce for 15 minutes until the tomatoes break down, and some of the liquid has evaporated. Just before serving, sprinkle the sauce with the basil.

At the table, pass the freshly grated Parmesan so each person can help themselves.

2 tab vegetable or olive oil
½ Spanish onion, diced
4 cloves garlic, minced
1 28 oz can whole Italian tomatoes, chopped
2 tab capers
8 stuffed green olives, chopped
8 pitted black olives, chopped
¼ teas red pepper flakes (optional)
salt & pepper to taste
¼ cup fresh basil, roughly chopped
¼ cup freshly grated Parmesan

"Meaty" Sauce

Although this sauce doesn't contain a "meat" alternative, it has a "meaty" texture because of the addition of both sun-dried tomatoes and mushrooms. Chopping the vegetables uniformly will contribute to an even "meaty" texture for this sauce.

This is a quick sauce so make sure your pasta is boiling before you start.

> 5 minutes preparation
> 10 minutes cooking (approximately)
> Serves 4

Heat the oil in a large non-stick sauté pan over medium heat. Add the anchovies (If using) and sauté 30 seconds until the anchovies break apart. Add the garlic and onions and sauté a few minutes until the onion starts to brown.

Add the remaining ingredients except the tomato sauce and oregano. Stir to combine and sauté approximately 7minutes until the vegetables are cooked to your liking, stir periodically to ensure even cooking. When you're satisfied the vegetables are cooked, add the tomato sauce and oregano. Increase the heat slightly to bring the mixture to a boil. Stir and reduce to a simmer for a few more minutes and serve with your pasta.

> 2 heaping tablespoons vegetable oil
> 2 anchovy filets (optional)
> 2-3 large cloves garlic, finely chopped
> ½ large sweet onion, finely diced

¼ medium sweet pepper, finely chopped
4-5 sun-dried tomatoes in oil (remove oil using paper towels), finely chopped
1-tab banana peppers rings, finely diced (optional)
½ cup finely chopped mushrooms
½ medium zucchini, finely chopped
½ teas dried oregano
1 19 oz can tomato sauce

Mushroom Lasagna

This lasagna is a little more complex with the addition of a mushroom layer. It is my version "company" lasagna, for special occasions.

½ hour preparation
1 hour baking at 350°
8 servings

Pre-heat the oven to 350°. Spray a large lasagna dish with vegetable cooking spray and set aside.

Prepare the lasagna as the package directs. Place the cooked pasta in a colander and rinse with cold water. Dry each noodle with paper towel. Place each noodle side by side on a large piece of waxed paper. Make sure the noodles don't overlap so they don't stick together.

In a large non-stick sauté pan, over medium-low heat sauté the onions in the butter until softened. Stir in the mushrooms and sauté for 3-5 minutes. Stir in the remaining sauce ingredients and reduce the heat and simmer for 15 minutes.

In a large bowl, combine all the ingredients for the spinach layer.

Pour a thin layer of the tomato mushroom sauce into the bottom of the lasagna dish. Add a layer of cooked noodles. Spread ½ of the remaining tomato mushroom sauce over the noodles, and spread evenly with all the spinach mixture. Top with another layer of noodles. Cover the noodles completely with the remaining tomato mushroom sauce.

Sprinkle the surface with the combined cheeses. Cover the dish with foil and bake at 350° for 50-60 minutes until bubbling.

Allow the baked lasagna to cool for 15 minutes to ½ hour before serving. You will find it firms up and will be easier to serve in slices.

Quick Tip: Substitute 2 medium grated zucchini for the spinach layer for an interesting taste difference.

Tomato Mushroom Sauce:
2 tab butter
1 cup diced onion
2 cups fresh, diced mushrooms
15 oz can tomato sauce
5 ½ oz can tomato paste
1 teas dried oregano
1 teas salt
1 teas sugar
1 tab dried basil

Spinach layer:
2 cups cottage cheese
1 egg
10 oz package frozen chopped spinach which has been de-frosted and drained

½ cup grated parmesan and 2 cups grated mozzarella combined in a bowl
salt, pepper & nutmeg to taste

1 package lasagna noodles—cooked as directed on the package

Mushroom Manicotti

Quick and easy to fill, Canneloni can be substituted for Manicotti if you would like to serve this as a pasta side dish. I find Manicotti easier to fill because they are bigger.

10 minutes preparation
8-10 minutes boiling pasta
30 minutes baking at 350°

Place the manicotti shells in a large pot of boiling, salted water. Boil until the pasta is cooked (usually 8-10 minutes).

Meanwhile, prepare the filling:
Sauté the mushrooms, onion, garlic and seasonings in a large non-stick sauté pan over medium heat until the onions are soft, about 5 minutes. Drain off some of the liquid created by the mushrooms, etc. Transfer contents to a large mixing bowl. Let cool 5 minutes before mixing in the drained cottage cheese and beaten egg.

Drain and dry the cooked manicotti with paper towels. Set aside. I place the manicotti on plastic wrap so it doesn't stick to anything. Using a parfait spoon (or any small spoon with a long handle), carefully spoon the filling into a manicotti tube. I usually fill one half, turn the tube around, and fill the other half. Don't pack it too tightly.

Using a rectangular baking dish or lasagna dish, pour enough of the tomato sauce on the bottom of the dish to cover it completely. Place each filled manicotti side by side until you're finished.

Cover the manicotti with all remaining tomato sauce. Sprinkle the surface with the red chili flakes if you're using them. Cover completely with the cheddar cheese. Fill in any gaps with the Parmesan. Place on a baking sheet and bake at 350° for 30 minutes or until the filling is bubbly.

Cool at least 10 minutes before serving so it holds together.

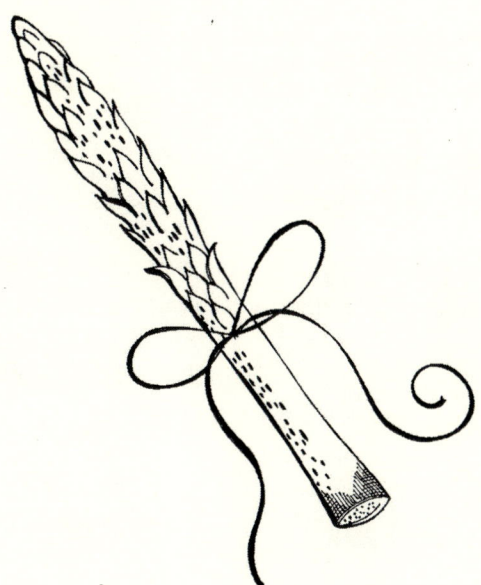

Cooking Tip: if you find it too difficult to fill the manicotti using a spoon, cut the manicotti down one side using scissors. Lay flat. Fill then roll and place seam down in the baking dish.

Filling:
2 tabs vegetable oil
1 package Cremini (or other) mushrooms, approx. 1 lb, diced
½ sweet onion, finely diced
3 large cloves garlic, finely chopped
1 tab oregano
salt & pepper to taste
½ teaspoon dried or fresh thyme (if fresh, leaves only, finely chopped)

1 container cottage cheese, drained*
1 egg, beaten

Sauce:
1 large (26 oz) can tomato sauce
sprinkle of red chili flakes (optional)
1 cup grated cheddar mild or medium
3-4 tablespoons freshly grated Parmesan

8-10 manicotti pasta shells (you only need 8, but boil 10 in case you have extra filling or 2 shells tear when preparing)**

* this is a very important step—drain the container of cottage cheese by emptying the contents into a strainer set over a bowl. Drain for 10 minutes, but ½ hour would be better if you have the time.
Removing the excess liquid will result in a firmer filling for your manicotti (the filling won't ooze out when its cut).

Mushroom Sauce

If you're using Shitake mushrooms, remove the woody stems before using. If you use dried mushrooms, soak them in boiling water for 10 minutes before using—the soaking water will contain a lot of flavor, so add it to your stock.

10-minutes preparation
10 minutes cooking
4 servings

In a large non-stick sauté pan, melt the butter and oil over medium heat. Add the mushrooms and sauté a few minutes until they release their juices. Add the red pepper, and sauté a couple of minutes. Add the remaining ingredients except the Parmesan. When the sauce reaches a simmer, add the Parmesan and stir until incorporated.

Serve the mushroom sauce over cooked pasta. Garnish with freshly chopped basil. Season with salt and pepper.

Quick Tip: Buy vegetable stock cubes and dissolve them in boiling water to make a stock. Use slightly less water if you want a stronger flavor.

2 tab butter
2 tab olive oil
6 cups assorted wild mushrooms (Oyster, Shitake, Portobello), sliced

¼ sweet red pepper, diced
1 dried chili pepper
1 cup vegetable stock
¾ cup heavy cream
2 tab fresh lemon juice
½ teas dried thyme

¾ cup parmesan, grated

Garnish:
Fresh Basil—approx 4-5 large leaves, chopped

Salt & pepper to taste

Pasta Salad

I often make a cold salad during the hot summer months when we don't want a heavy meal. You can bump up the protein content by adding a little more cheese and a couple of cold, hard-boiled eggs, chopped.

10 minutes preparation
10 minutes (pasta cooking)
4 servings

Cook pasta, cool and drain. Place it in a large salad bowl. Add the salad ingredients and toss to combine.

In a small bowl, whisk together the dressing ingredients. Taste the dressing and adjust if necessary (by adding more oil if too acidic, or more vinegar if too oily). Quickly add the whisked dressing to the salad bowl and toss to combine. Cover and chill for a few hours (or overnight) for the flavors to combine.

Just before serving, garnish with fresh parmesan and season with herbs and salt & pepper.

Variation: Garnish with freshly chopped mint instead of basil for a different flavor

Quick Tip: When in season, substitute fresh asparagus for green beans.

¼ sweet red pepper, julienne
4 large stuffed green olives, sliced
1 tab capers

LAUREEN OSBORNE

½ lb green beans, cooked, cooled and cut into 1" pieces

2 small jars marinated artichoke hearts—drained, cut into bite size pieces
¼ red onion, thinly sliced
2 tab chopped hot banana pepper rings (optional)
2 tab feta cheese, crumbled

Dressing:
2 tab red or white wine vinegar
juice from ½ lemon (or to taste)
½ tab Dijon mustard
1 tab olive oil

salt & pepper to taste
fresh parsley & basil to taste
fresh parmesan to taste

Cooked pasta shapes (such as fusilli or penne)

Pesto Sauce

You can also make this sauce with either dill or coriander instead of basil. You can substitute toasted walnut pieces, or toasted raw unsalted sunflower seeds for the pine nuts—experiment and see what combinations you like best!

10 minutes preparation
4-6 servings

Put all the ingredients in the food processor and process until it forms a thick paste. Taste and adjust the seasonings.

Serve over spaghetti, spagettini or capellini

Quick Tip: freeze pesto in ice cube trays. When frozen, transfer the cubes to a freezer bag. Each cube is approx. one serving.

LAUREEN OSBORNE

4 cups fresh basil leaves, stems removed
2 cloves fresh garlic
½ cup grated Parmesan
2 tab toasted pine nuts
zest of one lemon
½ cup olive oil
a couple dashes hot sauce (optional)
pinch of coarse salt & pepper to taste

Rose Sauce

I like to use sun-dried tomatoes that are preserved in oil. Remove what you need from the oil, and lay each tomato on a piece of paper towel. Blot completely to remove all the excess oil then thinly slice them (chiffonade). You can also use dried sun-dried tomatoes but they have to be re-hydrated by soaking in boiling water for 10 minutes, so that adds to your preparation time.

10-minutes preparation
10 minutes cooking
4 servings

Sauté the garlic and onion in the oil for a few minutes. Add the sun-dried tomatoes, tomatoes and tomato paste and sauté another 2-5 minutes until the fresh tomatoes start to dissolve. Add the vegetable stock and heat to a simmer. Slowly pour in the cream and stir to combine. Let thicken slightly. Once the sauce is thoroughly heated, taste it and season with salt and pepper.

Pour the sauce over cooked pasta of your choice. Garnish each serving with pine nuts, basil and parmesan.

1 large clove garlic, crushed
½ cup finely diced sweet onion
2 tab olive oil
3-4 sun-dried tomatoes, chiffonade
2 medium tomatoes, cored & diced
1 tab tomato paste
¼ cup vegetable stock
¼ cup 18% cream

LAUREEN OSBORNE

salt & pepper to taste

Garnish:
2 tab toasted pine nuts
fresh basil (4-5 leaves, chopped)
freshly grated parmesan (2-3 tab)

Pasta (prepared as package directs)

Spinach Lasagna

Its always a good idea to place your lasagna dish on top of a cookie sheet in the oven, in case the sauce bubbles over.

This lasagna uses mostly cheddar cheese instead of the traditional mozzarella. I prefer the stronger cheddar flavor, which gives the lasagna a bit of "bite."

15-minutes preparation
35-45 minutes baking at 350º
8 servings

Pre-heat the oven to 350º.

Spray your lasagna dish with vegetable cooking spray (don't forget the sides and the handles!). Add enough tomato sauce to the bottom of the dish to cover it completely. Lay 3 cooked lasagna noodles side by side, on top of the sauce.

Sauté the onions, mushrooms and garlic in oil until lightly browned. Transfer this mixture to a large bowl. Add the spinach, cottage cheese, basil and oregano to the bowl. Mix well. Spread about half the mixture evenly over the first layer of noodles in the dish. Cover this layer with three more noodles. Add the rest of the mixture from the bowl, and spread evenly over the noodles. Cover this layer with the last three noodles. Cover the noodles with the remaining tomato sauce; making sure the lasagna is completely covered. Sprinkle the surface with red pepper flakes (if you're using them).

In a medium bowl, combine the cheeses. Sprinkle evenly over the surface of the lasagna. Bake in a pre-heated 350° oven for 35-45 minutes until the sauce is bubbling.

9 cooked and cooled lasagna noodles
28 oz canned or fresh tomato sauce
1 Spanish onion, finely chopped
½ cup mushrooms, chopped
2-3 large cloves garlic, finely chopped
¼ cup olive or vegetable oil
½ package frozen chopped spinach—defrosted in the microwave & drained (approx 1 cup when prepared)
1 carton cottage cheese (500 g)
¼ cup chopped fresh basil
1 tab dried oregano
Dried red pepper flakes to taste (try ¼ teas) (optional)

2 cups grated cheddar (mild or medium)
¼ cup grated Parmesan
1 cup grated mozzarella

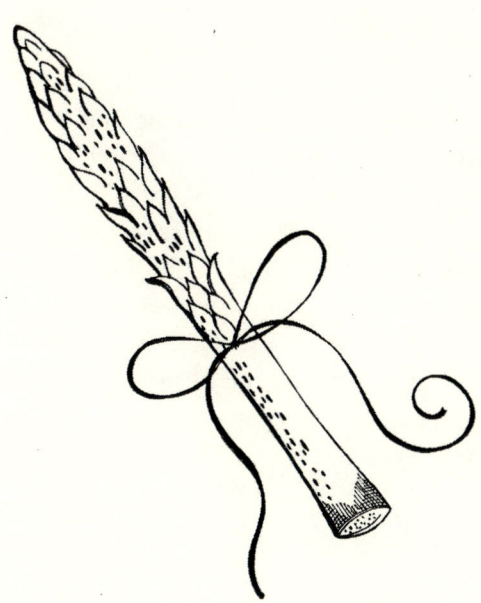

Quick Tip: Cook your lasagna noodles first. Rinse them under cold water and pat them dry with paper towel. Place them side-by-side on a large sheet of waxed paper. Now they won't stick together and will be easier to handle.

Introduction to Eggs & Cheese

Eggs

When you walk in the door at night and you've got to get a meal on the table in a hurry, remember eggs!—scrambled, poached or with baked beans and cooked vegetables, and you're in business. Always keep a few frozen pie shells on hand so that you can make a quick quiche and salad. Use any leftover cooked vegetables and potatoes to make an omelet or frittata.

If you want to boost the nutritional value of a dish, think eggs. Eggs contain the highest quality source of protein available. In addition, they also contain 13 essential vitamins (including Vitamin D) and minerals needed for a healthy diet.

A large size egg is only 75 calories.

All the fat and cholesterol in eggs is found in the yolks. All the protein is found in the whites.

Eggs can be cooked many different ways, go with a lot of different foods and cook fast. Don't forget to add hard-boiled eggs to your salads and potato salad.

Cheese

Cheese is another "Protein Powerhouse"—a 2-oz/50 g serving of cheddar cheese has as much protein as two large eggs. Because cheese is made from milk, it also contains a lot of calcium.

Generally, "hard" cheeses are higher in cholesterol than "soft" cheeses. Low fat cheese is lower in cholesterol than regular cheese. Read the package to determine how much cholesterol is present.

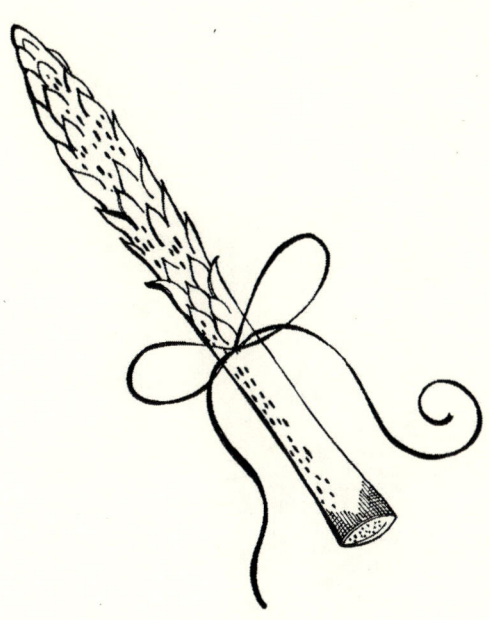

Researchers still aren't sure if there is a direct link between dietary cholesterol and blood cholesterol.

Egg and Cheese: Recipes

Cheese Quesadillas

This is basically a Mexican grilled cheese, and it's really easy to make. Choose small or medium size tortillas otherwise you may have difficulty flipping them over when the time comes.

They are good with a little homemade (or store-bought) salsa and/or guacamole on the side.

5 minutes preparation
20 minutes (approx) frying time

Assemble each quesadilla just before frying. Put the cheese, onions and peppers each in individual bowls. Put one tortilla on a plate. Sprinkle grated cheese over the tortilla (avoid putting the cheese too close to the edge of the tortilla or it may fall out when you transfer it to the pan). Sprinkle it with onions and hot peppers. Lay another tortilla on top. This is one quesadilla.

Drizzle a thin layer of oil into a large non-stick sauté pan. Place the pan on medium-high heat and heat until quite hot but not smoking. Using a large non-stick spatula, transfer the quesadilla to your sauté pan. Slip the quesadilla into the pan, being careful not to splash yourself with the hot oil. Using your spatula, press all over the top of the tortilla to help melt the cheese. Fry for a couple of minutes. Using your spatula, lift the edge of the tortilla to look at the bottom. It should be golden brown and a little crispy. If it isn't, fry for 30 seconds more. Using your spatula, lift the quesadilla out of the pan and carefully flip it over to fry the other side. Press this side all over with the spatula. When this side is golden brown, transfer the quesadilla to a paper towel to absorb the excess oil from frying. Use another paper towel to pat the top layer of the quesadilla to remove excess oil. Prepare each quesadilla this way.

Cut each quesadilla into four wedges and serve on a plate with salsa and/or guacamole on the side.

Variation: add a thin layer of mashed, re-fried beans to the tortilla before adding the cheese.

Variation: substitute sliced green or black olives for the jalapenos or banana peppers if you don't want your quesadillas to be too spicy

1 cup grated medium or mild cheddar cheese (Use approx ¼ cup per quesadilla)
4-6 green onions*, thinly sliced
3-4 slices of pickled jalapeno peppers or hot banana pepper rings per quesadilla (optional)
1-package small or medium size fresh soft tortillas
vegetable oil for the pan

*if you don't have any green onions, you can used very thinly sliced sweet onion—approx ¼ cup for four quesadillas

Egg Foo Young

Like most stir-fry dishes, this one is fast and easy. You can also try making it with shredded Nappa cabbage instead of bean sprouts.

Spread the egg mixture up the side of your wok so that it cooks quickly and evenly. This dish is good with or without the added sauce. If you're serving it with a selection of other stir-fried dishes, you may not need the extra flavor provided by the sauce.

10 minutes total time (including preparation and stir-frying)
4 servings

Put enough oil in the wok to coat the bottom (approx 1 1/2 tab). Heat on high heat. When hot, add the bean sprouts and quickly stir-fry for a minute or two (just until they start to soften). When they are ready, you can either remove them to a separate plate, or push them to the side so that you can add the eggs.

Add the beaten eggs to the bottom of the wok, and try to coat the wok up the sides with the egg. Let sit for approx. 30 seconds until you can see the egg starting to solidify. Give the wok a tilt so more of the uncooked egg spreads up the sides of the wok. When the egg is pretty much set, use a large spatula or wok strainer and turn the eggs over (don't worry if you can't flip it all in one piece). Cook the other side. When it is set, use the edge of your spatula or strainer to cut the egg into strips. Incorporate the bean sprouts back into the wok and mix the whole thing together with 1 tab soy sauce.

Create an opening in the center of the bean sprout-egg mixture in the bottom of your wok. Pour in the diluted sauce. When the sauce boils, add the liquid cornstarch and stir quickly until the sauce thickens. Mix the sauce into the bean sprout/egg mixture. Garnish the whole thing with green onions and serve immediately.

Oil for the pan
4 eggs, beaten in a medium bowl with salt, pepper and 1-2 teas curry powder
4 servings bean sprouts, rinsed
1 tab soy sauce

Sauce Options: Choose one. In a small bowl combine 2 tab sauce diluted with ¼ cup water:

Black Bean Sauce
Oyster Sauce
Stir Fry Sauce
Ginger Sauce

1 heaping tablespoon cornstarch dissolved in (approx 2 tab) water to form a thick liquid

Garnish:
4 green onions, sliced on the diagonal

Eggs Benedict

Eggs aren't just for breakfast. It's true. This dish is rich and elegant. The hollandaise sauce matches beautifully with a side of steamed asparagus or leeks*.

Preparation time: 10 minutes using a double boiler
4 servings

You can make your own double boiler by setting a large stainless steel mixing bowl over a medium saucepan that has 2" of water in the bottom. The mixing bowl should be larger than the saucepan and you want to ensure the bottom of the bowl touches the water.

Over medium heat, melt the butter in the top of the double boiler. Add the flour and whisk to make a thick paste. Whisk in the hot water, until the mixture is slightly thick.

Add the salt, pepper and lemon juice. In a separate bowl, beat the egg yolks. Pour the yolks into the top of the double boiler. Wearing oven mitts, hold the edge of the bowl and whisk the mixture constantly until a creamy sauce develops. Sprinkle with cayenne or paprika. If you would like a richer flavor, add another egg yolk.

Put one poached egg on half of a toasted English muffin. Pour a quarter of the hollandaise sauce over. Do this with each egg until you have prepared four servings.

Variation: Steam a package of fresh chopped spinach for a few minutes. Put the drained spinach on the muffin before adding the poached egg, then add the sauce.

Variation: Slice a large beefeater tomato and fry lightly in a little oil or butter in a small sauté pan. Place the slice of tomato on top of the muffin, top with the poached egg. Add 1 thin slice Gruyere or Gouda cheese before topping with sauce. The warm sauce will help to melt the cheese.

Hollandaise Sauce:
2 tab flour
3 tab butter
1 cup hot water
½ teas salt & pepper
2 tab fresh lemon juice
3 egg yolks
dash cayenne pepper or paprika

4 toasted English muffins
4 poached eggs**

*It can be difficult to get leeks clean. Chop the leek widthwise where the green meets the white. Discard the excess green. Slice lengthwise from approx. 1" from the root to the end of the leek. Turn the leek on its side and slice again. The stalk is now in four long strips, but still attached to the bulb. Run the strips under cold water and rinse each layer, removing any dirt or sand.

**If you don't have an egg poacher, boil the eggs in water. Break each egg into a bowl, being careful to keep the yolk intact. Put a ½" of water in a sauté pan and bring to the boil. Gently slide the egg into the pan. Reduce the heat to simmer and leave the egg until it reaches the desired degree of hardness. Using a spatula, Carefully remove the egg from the water. Place the egg on a piece of paper towel to remove the excess water.

Huevos Rancheros

This is a dish I first tasted in Mexico. Serve with hash browns or roasted potatoes and a salad for a quick, nutritious meal.

10 minutes preparation
4 servings

Add the oil to a large non-stick sauté pan. Add the garlic and onion and sauté over medium-low heat for a few minutes until the onion starts to brown. Add the tomatoes and seasonings and sauté for another few minutes until the tomatoes start to break up.

Pour the beaten eggs over the tomato/onion mixture. Cover the pan with a lid and cook over medium-low heat until the eggs have set to your liking (approx 8 to 10 minutes).

Variation: to make this a "Mexican" meal, serve with refried beans instead of hash browns.
Variation: for additional flavor and color, when you add the onions, you can add a quarter of a finely diced sweet red or green pepper.

2 tab oil
1 large clove garlic, smashed and chopped
½ sweet onion, finely diced
1 cup chopped fresh tomatoes
1 tab chili powder
1 teas oregano

LAUREEN OSBORNE

4 eggs, beaten in a medium bowl and seasoned with salt and pepper

Garnish (optional):
a little chopped fresh cilantro

"Italian" Style Eggs

You can serve these eggs with a little cooked pasta such as fettuccine. I prefer to keep it light, and just serve them with a green salad made with arugula.

5 minutes preparation
15 minutes cooking
4-6 servings

Using a large, non-stick sauté pan, fry the garlic in olive oil over medium heat. Add the tomatoes. Season with salt, pepper and a pinch of sugar. Simmer for a few minutes to allow the flavor to develop.

Make four spaces in the tomato mixture, one for each egg. Place the eggs evenly apart so they don't touch as they're cooking. Season each egg with salt, pepper and a little red pepper flakes (if using).

Cover the pan and simmer until the eggs are set (this will take approx. 8-10 minutes). When the eggs are done to your liking, sprinkle each of the eggs with a little Parmesan.

Using a large spoon, carefully lift out each egg (and some of the tomato mixture), onto each plate. Garnish each plate with a little fresh basil and serve immediately.

2 tab olive oil
2 cloves garlic, thinly sliced
1 19 oz can Italian plum tomatoes (chopped)
salt & pepper to taste
pinch of sugar

LAUREEN OSBORNE

4 to 6 large eggs
pinch of red pepper flakes (optional)

¼ cup freshly grated Parmesan cheese

Garnish:
2 stalks fresh basil, leaves removed and chopped

Mushroom Frittata

The crust is optional, but it adds a delicious texture. Serve the frittata with a mixed green salad or cooked vegetable (such as green beans or asparagus). Serve the salad or veggies with mustard vinaigrette*.

You can substitute other vegetables for the mushrooms, such as broccoli, zucchini, sweet peppers—just make sure you cook them before adding to the crust.

15 minutes preparation
20 minutes cooking time
4 servings

Start the crust first and while its frying, prepare the other ingredients.

Combine the grated potato and onion in a large colander. Pat the mixture with a paper towel if it is particularly wet (removing the moisture will give you a crispier crust).

Pre-heat a large non-stick skillet with 1 tab vegetable oil. Using a large, non-stick spatula, transfer the potato mixture to the pan. Spread it evenly, making sure there are no holes so that the potato mixture will form a thin crust. Fry slowly (medium-low heat) for approx. 5 minutes. Using your spatula, carefully, turn the mixture over and fry the other side. Keep turning every five minutes until the potato is cooked and has made a crispy crust.

Meanwhile, in a separate skillet gently sauté the mushrooms in oil until cooked (medium-low heat 3-5 min). Sprinkle with the chopped thyme. Set aside.

When the crust is cooked, distribute the cooked mushrooms over the top. Pour the beaten eggs over the whole mixture and tilt the pan slightly so that the eggs cover the entire surface. Sprinkle with the grated cheese.

Cover the skillet with a lid and cook until the eggs are set and the cheese has melted (approx. another five minutes using medium heat).

Carefully slide the frittata out of the pan and onto a cutting board. Cut into four wedges.

Crust:
1 baking potato—peeled and grated
2 tab grated onion (about ½ small onion)

1 tab vegetable oil

Filling:
1 tab vegetable oil
2 cups assorted wild mushrooms—cleaned with a paper towel, tough stems removed and thinly sliced
2 sprigs fresh thyme, stripped from their branches and finely chopped

3 eggs beaten in a medium bowl with ½ teas chili powder and ½ teas dried oregano
¾ cup grated cheddar (medium or old)

*Mustard Vinaigrette:

1 teas Dijon mustard
2 tab tarragon vinegar
3-4 tab olive oil
½ clove garlic—very finely minced
salt and pepper to taste

Put mustard, vinegar and garlic in medium sized glass or ceramic bowl. Whisk to combine. Gradually add 3 tab oil, whisking constantly. Taste it and add the last tab of oil to the dressing if the flavor is too vinegary for you. Season with salt & pepper.

Mushroom Quiche

The secret to this recipe is the slow sauté of the onions. They become "caramelized" and impart a delicious flavor to the quiche.

If you like your quiche to be more "eggy," add an extra whole egg. I just like to add enough eggs to hold the filling together.

10 minutes preparation
15 minutes cooking
35 minutes baking at 350^0
4-6 servings

Heat the oil in a large sauté pan. Add the onions. Sprinkle with the vinegar. Sauté the onions slowly until caramelized, about 10 minutes. Add the mushroom slices, and sauté another 5 minutes.

Place mixture in the bottom of a baked pie crust. Sprinkle with the cheeses. Beat the eggs and cream together in a small bowl. Pour over the pie ingredients. Sprinkle the fresh herbs on top and season with salt & pepper.

Bake 350° for 30 minutes until firm.

Serve with a green salad.

Variation: For a more complex flavor, add a little crumbled feta or Parmesan cheese when you add the herbs.

Variation: Add ½ small sliced zucchini when you add the mushroom slices, making this a vegetable quiche.

VEGETARIAN FOR A DAY

Tip: for a nicer presentation, thinly slice a small tomato on top of the cooked quiche and brown under the broiler before serving.

2 tab olive oil
½ large sweet onion, sliced thinly
1 tab Balsamic vinegar
1½ lb sliced mushrooms (wild preferred*)

1 baked pie shell
½ cup shredded mild cheese (brick, mozzarella, etc)
½ cup shredded medium cheddar

2 tab crumbled feta (optional) or
2 tab freshly grated parmesan (optional)

2 eggs, beaten
½ cup half & half cream
1 sprig fresh thyme**
½ teas dried tarragon or oregano

*A mixture of Porcini and fresh Shitake mushrooms will give the most flavor
**Hold a sprig of thyme by the tip and put your index and thumb on either side of the stalk. Quickly run your two fingers down the stem and the tiny leaves will fall off. Chop the leaves with a sharp knife. Discard the stalk.
Fresh thyme stalks are even easier to strip if they have been frozen first.

Paneer with Spinach

Paneer is fresh cheese made from yoghurt. Paneer is found in Indian grocery stores. It is usually sold in vacuum-sealed blocks (similar to the way tofu is packaged). You can use pressed Ricotta if you can't find paneer.

This is my favorite paneer dish. I've also made it with beet greens. The flavor is a little stronger.

10 minutes preparation
10 minutes frying (Paneer)
10 minutes cooking
4 servings

Thoroughly wash the fresh spinach. Use a large metal bowl and fill it with cold water. Add each piece of spinach as it is removed from the stem (big stems can be cut away from the leaves with scissors). As the bowl start to fill with spinach, swish it around and rub the leaves together to remove any dirt or grit. When all the spinach is added, hold the spinach and pour off the water. Refill the bowl with water and swish and rub the spinach a couple of more times until the bottom of the bowl has no trace of sand (You won't enjoy eating gritty spinach, so make sure its well washed). Set the spinach aside.

In a large non-stick sauté pan, add enough oil to coat the bottom. Heat to medium low then add the diced onions. Sauté for a few minutes until the onion is tender. Add the garlic and chili pepper and seasonings and sauté for a minute longer.

Using tongs, remove the spinach from the bowl of water, and lay it across the onion mixture in the sauté pan (do NOT shake the water off the spinach pieces, this water will help to steam the spinach). When all the spinach has been added, cover the pan and steam for a few minutes. Take the lid off and taste a piece of spinach (run it under cold water first so you don't burn your mouth). If it's cooked to your liking, stir the spinach gently into the onion mixture (if its not cooked enough, give it another minute with the lid on). Once combined, add the bottled sauce and gently add the fried pieces of Paneer. Cover the pan again and cook for a few minutes until the sauce has heated.

Serve with plain white rice.

1 large bunch fresh spinach, stems removed
2-3 tab vegetable oil
½ sweet onion, diced
2-3 large cloves garlic, minced
1 green chili pepper* finely diced (optional)
1 tab ground cumin
1 tab ground coriander seeds

1 bottle mild Indian curry sauce Korma or Balti, (look for coconut in the ingredient list, it goes well with spinach)

1 package Paneer, cut into bite-sized cubes and fried in a little oil and drained*

*You can buy Paneer that has already been fried but I prefer to do it myself. Using a large non-stick saucepan, heat about 3 tab vegetable oil on medium-high heat until hot. Using long-handled tongs, carefully add the pieces of Paneer and fry on all sides until golden brown (each side should only take a minute or less). Using your tongs, carefully remove each piece and drain on paper towel to remove the excess oil.

*Quick Tip: Fresh hot peppers will be less hot if you remove the seeds before using. Always wear gloves when handling hot peppers!

Potato and Onion Frittata

This is a simple frittata using only a few ingredients. You can try different combinations but always use the eggs and cheese to hold the whole thing together.

This is a good way to use leftover potatoes and cooked vegetables. Serve with a salad.

10 minutes preparation
18 minutes cooking
2 minutes cooling
4-6 servings

Pour the oil into a large, non-stick sauté pan. Heat on medium-low. Add the potatoes and sprinkle with the bowl of seasoning. Sauté until golden brown (approx 10 minutes). When sautéed, spread the potatoes evenly over the bottom of the pan.

While the potatoes are cooking, use a separate sauté pan, over low heat to sauté the onions and vinegar in oil. Sauté for the same length of time as the potatoes. Add the onions to the cooked potatoes that are already in the other pan.

In a bowl, combine the eggs with the cheese and pour over the entire pan of potatoes and onions. Tilt the pan to ensure all the egg/cheese mixture comes in contact with the potato/onion mixture. Cover the pan with a lid and cook for 7 to 8 minutes or until the egg/cheese mixture is set.

Remove the lid and let cool for 2 minutes. Using a large, non-stick spatula, carefully loosen the frittata from the edges of the pan. Give the pan a shake to see if frittata moves freely. If it does, slide the frittata out of the pan and onto your cutting board. If it's sticking, carefully run your spatula under the frittata to loosen. Cut into 4 or 6 slices (like a pie) and serve warm or cold.

Cooking Tip: if your sauté pan didn't come with a lid, use the lid from your Dutch oven or wok. If that doesn't work, you can always cover your pan with a sheet of tin foil.

Variation: Instead of covering the pan and cooking on the stove top, the frittata can be broiled in the oven. After covering the potatoes with the egg/cheese mixture, place the pan* in the oven on the middle rack and set the oven to broil. Keep an eye on it so it doesn't burn. Broil until the egg is set and the cheese has melted.

Variation: just before broiling, sprinkle the top with 1 oz of feta cheese, crumbled and 4 or 5 sliced black olives. Broil as above.

*If you're not sure the handle of your sauté pan is oven-proof, cover the entire handle with tinfoil to protect it from the heat.

2 tab vegetable oil
1 baking potato—peeled, cubed and boiled
Combine in small bowl ½ teas each: chili powder, ground cumin, dried oregano, and garlic powder

½ Spanish onion, peeled and sliced
1 tab Balsamic vinegar

2 eggs, beaten
½ cup grated cheddar (medium)

Vegetarian for a Day

Once your family is enjoying one vegetarian meal a week, why not take the next step and be "vegetarian" for a day? Its easy! By having a breakfast of cereal or toast with fresh fruit, nuts or yoghurt, you'll be making a good start to the day. Next, pack those lunch boxes with pasta or bean salad, egg or cheese sandwiches and veggie snacks (like carrots or celery). Finally, for dinner, choose a delicious recipe from this book and sit down together and enjoy!

With a little planning, everyone can eat foods they love all day long, without eating meat. You may find that after a few weeks of being a Vegetarian for a Day, you feel better about your diet, and you feel better, period. There are so many times in our busy lives when we don't always feed ourselves nutritious foods. By eating vegetarian for one day a week, you'll be happy knowing you've made a healthy choice.

Becoming a Vegetarian

Many people feel tired after eating their main meal of the day. This is sometimes due to: improper calorie intake during the day (i.e. not getting enough nutrients to see you through until dinner time), over-eating because you are too hungry or stressed or eating foods (like meat), which are more difficult to digest.

Whether you choose to eat vegetarian for health or ethical reasons, its important to think of your diet throughout the day.

Success in becoming a vegetarian will depend on your interest in and willingness to eat different foods. Having a variety of foods to choose from prevents boredom because you're not always eating the same thing. It requires planning and an effort on your part to ensure you get the proper nutrients every day.

Eating out used to be a challenge for vegetarians. Most restaurants can now accommodate vegetarians. Choose an ethnic restaurant where vegetarianism is part of the culture. Asian or Indian restaurants are a good choice. You can also find vegetarian dishes at Italian and Mexican restaurants.

Eat "Mindfully." Try to think just about the food that is in front of you, don't eat while watching TV or talking; you won't be aware of how much you're eating if you are distracted. Really taste your food and enjoy every mouthful. Eat slowly so your stomach has the chance to tell your brain when you've had enough food.

Making the decision to eat healthy can lead to a healthy lifestyle, which includes exercise and stress reduction. When you exercise and work hard to stay in shape, you don't want to undo all your hard work by eating unhealthy foods—eating vegetarian will help you feel better.

It is my hope that you try more and more of these and other vegetarian recipes and you find yourself one day wanting to eat vegetarian all the time!

About the Author

Laureen Osborne has been a vegetarian since 1982.

She is the author of three books on dog grooming. This is her first cookbook.

Laureen works as a writer and editor. She is currently working on a series of children's books called "Backyard Friends," which are short stories about wild animals we see every day. She lives in Ottawa, Canada with her husband and two dogs.

Visit her website for more details: www.Larkspurpublications.com

Endnotes

1 Normal weight BMI range of 18.5 to 24.9 kg/m2
Overweight—BMI range of 25 to 29.9 kg/m2
Obese—BMI greater than 30 kg/m2

To calculate your own BMI, divide your weight in kilograms by your height in meters squared .

2 Current scientific evidence suggests just eating more vegetables and fruits could eliminate 20% of cancers. Improving diet and exercise alone could prevent 30-40% of all cancers.

3 Processed food is pre-packaged, prepared foods that are quicker to prepare. Processed foods generally have food additives such as preservatives, emulsifiers, flavorings and dyes (mostly chemicals). Try to eat whole foods instead—prepared fresh from "raw" ingredients

4 Years ago, Iodine was added to table salt to help prevent iodine deficiency (noticeably as a goiter or enlarged thyroid gland). Iodine occurs naturally in sea salt and sea salt also contains other useful trace minerals. Sea salt contains less sodium chloride than iodized salt and is unprocessed.

5 Marmite is a brown paste made from concentrated yeast extract. It tastes closest to concentrated boullion cubes and is very high in B12. Use sparingly.

6 We do know that many of the most popular pesticides used in agriculture are cancer causing, are toxic to the nervous system, cause skin, eye or lung irritation, can cause genetic damage and reproductive problems.

7 Applied to crops, the term refers to any genetic plant type that has had a gene or genes for a different species transferred into its genetic material using accepted techniques of genetic engineering. Opponents of GMOs say that scientists just don't know if they are harmful because they could cause problems that we haven't even thought of yet as a result of the infinite number of possible genetic transfers.

8 Calcium sulphate is also known as "gypsum" . Magnesium chloride is found in Nigari which in Japan is the liquid residue from concentration of sea water and crystallizing salt. Tofu made with calcium sulphate will contain more calcium than tofu made with nigari.

9 Except lasagna noodles—a little oil will prevent the noodles from sticking together in the pot

Bibliography and References

Bibliography

Books:

Bauer, Joy 2003,*The Complete Idiot's Guide to Total Nutrition*, Alpha Books, Indianapolis
Davis, Brenda & Vesanto, Melina, 2000, *Becoming Vegan*, Book Publishings Company, Summertown, Tenn.
Moore Lappe, Frances, 1991, *Diet for a Small Planet*, Ballantine Books, New York
Schwartz, Rosie, 2003, *The Enlightened Eater's Whole Foods Guide*, Viking Canada, Toronto
Editors, Vegetarian Times, and Moll, Lucy, 1995, *Vegetarian Times Complete Cookbook*, MacMillan, New York

Articles:
Posluns, Elaine, BASc, RD, August 2000, *Hotspot The ABCs of Vitamins and Minerals*

Websites:

Are Raw vegetables always better for you, viewed December 17, 2006, http://www.healthandgoodness.com/nutritiondiet/RawCooked.htm
Are there any cheeses that are low in cholesterol?, viewed January 14, 2007, http://nutrition.about.com/od/askyournutritionist/f/lowcholcheese.htm
Basic Seitan, viewed December 17, 2006, http://www.innerself.com/recipes/entrees/seitan.htm

Basil Chiffonade, (Orlando Sentinel), viewed July 2, 2007, http://www.dailypress.com/features/food/orl-cooking-class-chiffonade,0,1619363.column

Canada's Guidelines for Healthy Eating Queen Elizabeth II Health Sciences Centre, October, 1997

Cheese & Health, viewed January 14, 2007, http://www.richesmonts.com/page_en/from_san/cheese_hea.html

Dietary Guidelines, viewed November 18, 2006, http://www.mypyramid.gov/guidelines/index.html

Eating vegetables raw is better than cooked, March 21, 2005, viewed December 17, 2006, http://www.foodsnherbs.com/new_page_3.htm

Expert Cooking Definitions Tips, viewed July 2, 2007, http://cooking.lifetips.com/cat/64184/cooking-definitions/index.html

Fresh, dried pasta differ but equal, Marcus, Erica, November 30, 2006 viewed December 9, 2006, http://www.sun-sentinel.com/features/food/sfl-pastquestnov30,0,113052.story?coll=sfla-features-food

Glorious Grains Guide, viewed January 14, 2007, http://www.foodfit.com/healthy/healthyGrains.asp

Legumes: Using Beans, Peas and Lentils instead of Meat, Mayo Clinic Staff, June 17, 2005 viewed October 23, 2006, http://www.mayoclinic.com/health/legumes/NU00260

Nutrient Value of Cheese, viewed January 14, 2007, http//www.dairygoodness.ca/en/Consumers/Products/Cheese/DairyFactsAndFallacies.htm

Nutrient Value of Eggs, viewed January 14, 2007, http://www.enc-online.org/eggnutr.htm

Organic Farming, Organic Alliance (www.organic.org) December 17, 2006, viewed December 17, 2006, http://www.tricountyfarm.org/oregon_organic.asp

Pasta Nutrition Feeney, Mary Jo, MS, RD, FADA, viewed December 9, 2006, http://www.ilovepasta.org/nutrition.html

Rice, White Rice, Couscous, viewed April 15, 2007. http://en.wikipedia.org/wiki/Rice, http://enwikipedia.org/wiki/White_rice, http://en.wikipedia/org/wiki/Couccous

Rice and Human Nutrition, http://www.faoorg/rice2004/en/factsheets.htm

Simple vs. Complex Carbohydrates, viewed December 9, 2006, http://www.ivillage.co.uk/print/0,,156580,00.html

Tempeh viewed December 17, 2006, http://en.wikipedia.org/wiki/Tempeh

Tomatoes: cooked better than raw? April 23, 2002, viewed December 17, 2006, http://www.foodnavigator.com/news/ng.asp?id=43832-tomatoes-cooked-better

Vegetarian Dietary Sources, viewed October 23, 2006, http://www.vnv.org.au/Nutrition/Protein.htm

Vegetarian Food Pyramid, viewed May 11, 2006 http://www.vegsource.com/nutrition/pyramid.htm

What are GMO's (definition)?, Nafziger, Emerson, viewed December 17, 2006, http://web.aces.uiuc.edu/faq/faq.pdl?project_id=28&faq_id=583

What is Marmite? viewed Oct 20, 2006, http://www.spurgeon.org/~phil/marmite.htm

What is Tofu?, viewed October 13, 2006 http://www.soya.be/what-is-tofu.php

What is Wheat Germ? viewed April 15, 2007. http://www.wisegeek.com/what-is-wheat-germ.htm

Wild Rice, viewed January 14, 2007, http://en.wikipedia.org/wiki/Wild_rice